US Edition 2004 - 2005

ISAF Special Regulations Governing Offshore and Oceanic Equipment and Preparation
Including US SAILING Prescriptions

Terms Of Reference

The Special Regulations Sub-Committee was created by the newly formed Offshore Rule Co-ordinating Committee, later the ORC (Offshore Racing Council). As the horizons of offshore racing extended into round-the world and multihull activities, so too did the scope of Special Regulations, which now cover racing in six categories. A training section was introduced in 1999 and a Model Training Course (for which publications of RYA, AYF, and STCW were consulted) in 2003. A new liferaft standard (Appendix A Part II) was introduced in 2002, and adopted by governmental authorities in Australia and the UK. Inshore requirements (Appendix J) were added in 2003. Special Regulations are continuously reviewed and re-published biennially.

Interpretations, amendments, and also extract files for particular categories and boat types, are available on the web site below. Assistance from Bob McPherson in computer programming is gratefully acknowledged.

In the US proposed changes to these regulations should be submitted in writing to the Director of Offshore Sailing at the US Sailing Association.

Extract files with US SAILING prescriptions added are available at www.ussailing.org/safety.

Contact Details for the ISAF Secretariat:
ISAF (UK) Ltd.
Ariadne House, Town Quay, Southampton SO14 2AQ
tel +44 (0) 2380 635111 fax +44 (0) 2380 63 5789
Email: secretariat@isaf.co.uk
Web Site: http://www.sailing.org.

Publication's title and number:

US Edition 2004 - 2005
ISAF Special Regulations Governing
Offshore and Oceanic Equipment
Including US SAILING Prescriptions
(ISBN 0-9741058-5-6)

Issue Date: March 1, 2004

State Frequency: PUBLISHED IRREGULARLY

Authorized Organization's Name and Address
US SAILING
P.O. BOX 1260
15 MARITIME DRIVE
PORTSMOUTH, RI 02871
TEL: 401-683-0800
FAX: 401-683-0840
WEB: www.ussailing.org

Issue Number: ISSUE NO. 1

Designed and printed in the U.S.A. by Intrepid Design, 174 Bellevue Avenue, Suite 302
Newport, RI 02840 PHONE: 401-849-7499 FAX: 401-849-8699
info@MustHaveID.com   www.MustHaveID.com

US Edition 2004 - 2005

ISAF Special Regulations Governing Offshore and Oceanic Equipment and Preparation

Including US SAILING Prescriptions

US SAILING

US Edition 2004 - 2005

ISAF Special Regulations Governing Offshore and Oceanic Equipment and Preparation
Including US SAILING Prescriptions

A Word From US SAILING

Dear U S Sailor,

These Special Regulations are the minimum safety standards of sailing carefully assembled by international and national Safety at Sea Committees in your behalf. These committees, made up of volunteers, represent you and your interests. If you see something in these standards that you disagree with let us know. Conversely, if something is missing or needs changing, let us know about it also.

In an attempt to make these regulations even more "user friendly" we are posting extracts of each of the six categories of races on the US SAILING web site at (www.ussailing.org/safety). Race Organizers should download the specific extract that they need and add, subtract or modify it for publication in their official race documents. Individual yacht owners should also use these extracts to outfit and prepare their yachts for both racing and cruising.

You will notice that there continues to be an emphasis on crew training in these regulations. The recent expansion of Section 6 has resulted in a complete revision of the curriculum of US SAILING's eight hour Safety at Sea Seminar program. There is also a new requirement for practical, hands-on training for offshore racers. US SAILING has placed the responsibility for this training directly on the skipper. Suggested topic outlines for this on board training have been prepared and are posted on the web site at (www.ussailing.org/safety).

Your opinion and suggestions are valuable to the people who administer the Safety at Sea program at US SAILING. Please let us know what you are thinking and how we can help you. You can contact us at offshore@ussailing.org.

The bottom line of all of this effort is that sailing should be not only safe but fun. We believe that Safe Sailors Have More Fun. We hope you agree.

Sail Safely,

Ronald C. Trossbach
Chairman, Safety at Sea Committee

ISAF Special Regulations Governing Offshore and Oceanic Equipment and Preparation
Including US SAILING Prescriptions

CONTENTS PAGE

SPECIAL REGULATIONS
JANUARY 2004 - DECEMBER 2005
©ORC Ltd. 2002, all amendments from 2003
©International Sailing Federation, (IOM) Ltd.
Reprinted with permission of
ISAF and ORC LTD. by
US SAILING ASSOCIATION
v 4.6

Notes to the 2004-2005 edition:

• A side bar indicates significant changes in 2004

• US SAILING extract files are available at the web site for individual categories and boat types (monohulls and multihulls) (**www.ussailing.org/safety/**)

• Official interpretations shall take precedence over these Special Regulations and will be indexed, numbered, dated and displayed on the ISAF web site **www.sailing.org**

Key to indices: Mo - Monohull, Mu - Multihull, ** means the item applies to all types of yacht in all Categories except 5. Category 5 Special Regulations are given in Appendix J.

• The use of the masculine gender shall be taken to mean either gender

• *Guidance notes and recommendations are in italics*

• ***US SAILING prescriptions are printed in bold, italic letters.***

ISAF Special Regulations Governing Offshore and Oceanic Equipment and Preparation
Including US SAILING Prescriptions

SECTION 1 - FUNDAMENTAL AND DEFINITIONS

		Category
1.01	**Purpose And Use**	
1.01.1	It is the purpose of these Special Regulations to establish uniform minimum equipment, accommodation and training standards for monohull and multihull yachts racing offshore. A Proa is excluded from these regulations.	**
1.01.2	These Special Regulations do not replace, but rather supplement, the requirements of governmental authority, the Racing Rules and the rules of Class Associations and Rating Systems. The attention of owners is called to restrictions in the Rules on the location and movement of equipment.	**
1.01.3	These Special Regulations, adopted internationally, are strongly recommended for use by all organizers of offshore races. Race Committees may select the category deemed most suitable for the type of race to be sailed.	**
1.02	**Responsibility of Person in Charge**	
1.02.1	The Safety of a yacht and her crew is the sole and inescapable responsibility of the owner, or owner's representative who must do his best to ensure that the yacht is fully found, thoroughly seaworthy and manned by an experienced crew who have undergone appropriate training and are physically fit to face bad weather. He must be satisfied as to the soundness of hull, spars, rigging, sails and all gear. He must ensure that all safety equipment is properly maintained and stowed and that the crew know where it is kept and how it is to be used.	**
1.02.2	Neither the establishment of these Special Regulations, their use by race organizers, nor the inspection of a yacht under these Special Regulations in any way limits or reduces the complete and unlimited responsibility of the owner or owner's representative.	**
1.02.3	**Decision to race -The responsibility for a yacht's decision to participate in a race or to continue racing is hers alone - RRS Fundamental Rule 4.**	
1.03	**Definitions, Abbreviations, Word Usage**	
1.03.1	Definitions of Terms used in this document	**

ISAF Special Regulations Governing Offshore and Oceanic Equipment and Preparation
Including US SAILING Prescriptions

Table 1

Age Date	Month/year of first launch
CEN	Comite European de Normalization
Coaming	Includes the transverse after limit of the cockpit over which water would run in the event that when the yacht is floating level the cockpit is flooded or filled to overflowing.
DSC	Digital Selective Calling
EN	European Norm
EPFS	Electronic Position-Fixing System
EPIRB	Electronic Position-Indicating Radio Beacon
FA station	The transverse station at which the upper corner of the transom meets the sheerline.
Foul-weather Suit	A foul weather suit is clothing designed to keep the wearer dry and may be either a jacket and trousers worn together, or a single garment comprising jacket and trousers.
GMDSS	Global Maritime Distress & Safety System
GPIRB	EPIRB, with integral GPS position-fixing
Hatch	The term hatch includes the entire hatch assembly and also the lid or cover as part of that assembly (the part itself may be described as a hatch).
IMO	International Maritime Organization
ISAF	International Sailing Federation.
ISO	International Standard or International Organization for Standardization.
Lifeline	(guardline) wire line rigged as guardrail around the deck
LOA	Length overall not including pulpits, bowsprits, boomkins etc.
LWL	(Length of) loaded waterline
Monohull	Yacht in which the hull depth in any section does not decrease towards the centre-line.
Permanently installed	Means the item is effectively built-in by eg bolting, welding, glassing etc. and may not be removed for or during racing.
PLB	Personal Locator Beacon
Proa	Asymmetric catamaran
RRS	ISAF - Racing Rules of Sailing
Series date	Month/year of first launch of the first yacht of the production series
SOLAS	Safety of Life at Sea Convention
Safety line	A tether used to connect a safety harness to a strong point
Securely fastened	Held strongly in place by a method (eg rope lashings, wing-nuts) which will safely retain the fastened object in severe conditions including a 180 degree capsize and allows for the item to be removed and replaced during racing.
Static safety line	A safety line (usually shorter than a safety line carried with a harness) kept clipped on at a work-station.

1.03.2	The words "shall" and "must" are mandatory, and "should" and "may" are permissive.	**
1.01.3	The word "yacht" shall be taken as fully interchangeable with the word "boat".	**

SECTION 2 - APPLICATION & GENERAL REQUIREMENTS

		Category
2.01	**Categories of events** *In many types of races, ranging from trans-oceanic sailed under adverse conditions to short-course day races sailed in protected waters, six categories are established, to provide for differences in the minimum standards of safety and accommodation required for such varying circumstances:*	**
2.01.1	**Category 0** Trans-oceanic races, including races which pass through areas in which air or sea temperatures are likely to be less than 5 degrees Celsius other than temporarily, where yachts must be completely self-sufficient for very extended periods of time, capable of withstanding heavy storms and prepared to meet serious emergencies without the expectation of outside assistance.	MoMu,0
2.01.2	**Category 1** *US SAILING prescribes that Category 1 races are of long distance, well offshore, in large unprotected bays, and in waters where large waves, strong currents, or conditions leading to rapid onset of hypothermia are possible, where yachts must be completely self-sufficient for extended periods of time, capable of withstanding heavy storms and prepared to meet serious emergencies without the expectation of outside assistance.*	MoMu,1
2.01.3	**Category 2** *US SAILING prescribes that Category 2 races are of extended duration along or not far removed from shorelines, where a high degree of self-sufficiency is required of the yachts but with the reasonable probability that outside assistance would be available for aid in the event of serious emergencies.*	MoMu,2
2.01.4	**Category 3** Races across open water, most of which is relatively protected or close to shorelines, including races for small yachts.	MoMu,3
2.01.5	**Category 4** Short races, close to shore in relatively warm or protected waters normally held in daylight.	MoMu,4
2.01.6	**Category 5 - for inshore racing** Please refer to Appendix J where Special Regulations for Category 5 are given in full. The symbol " ** " does not include Category 5.	
2.02	**Inspection** A yacht may be inspected at any time. If she does not comply with these Special Regulations her entry may be rejected, or she will be liable to disqualification or such other penalty as may be prescribed by the national authority or the race organizers.	**

		Category
2.03	**General Requirements**	
2.03.1	All equipment required by Special Regulations shall:-	
a)	function properly	**
b)	be regularly checked, cleaned and serviced	**
c)	when not in use be stowed in conditions in which deterioration is minimized	**
d)	be readily accessible	**
e)	be of a type, size and capacity suitable and adequate for the intended use and size of the yacht.	**
2.03.2	Heavy items:	
a)	ballast, ballast tanks and associated equipment shall be permanently installed	**
b)	heavy movable items including e.g. batteries, stoves, gas bottles, tanks, toolboxes and anchors and chain shall be securely fastened	**
c)	heavy items for which fixing is not specified in Special Regulations shall be permanently installed or securely fastened, as appropriate	**
2.03.3	When to show navigation lights	
a)	navigation lights (3.27) shall be shown as required by the International Regulations for Preventing Collision at Sea, (Part C and Technical Annex 1). All yachts shall exhibit sidelights and a sternlight at the required times.	**

SECTION 3 - STRUCTURAL FEATURES, STABILITY, FIXED EQUIPMENT

3.01	**Strength of build, ballast and rig**	
	Yachts shall be strongly built, watertight and, particularly with regard to hulls, decks and cabin trunks capable of withstanding solid water and knockdowns. They must be properly rigged and ballasted, be fully seaworthy and must meet the standards set forth herein. Shrouds shall never be disconnected.	**
3.02	**Watertight integrity of a hull**	
3.02.1	A hull, including, deck, coach roof, windows, hatches and all other parts, shall form an integral, essentially watertight unit and any openings in it shall be capable of being immediately secured to maintain this integrity.	**
3.02.2	Centerboard and daggerboard trunks and the like shall not open into the interior of a hull except via a watertight inspection/maintenance hatch of which the opening shall be entirely above the waterline of the yacht floating level in normal trim.	**

		Category
3.03	**Hull Construction Standards (Scantlings)**	

Table 2

LOA	Earliest of age or series date	
all	1/86 and after	MoMu0,1
12m (39.4 feet) and over	1/87 and after	MoMu2
under 12m (39.4 feet)	1/88 and after	MoMu2

3.03.1	A yacht defined in the table above shall have been designed and built in accordance with either:	MoMu0,1,2
a)	the EC Recreational Craft Directive for Category A (having obtained the CE mark), or	MoMu0,1,2
b)	the ABS Guide for Building and Classing Offshore Yachts in which case the yacht shall have on board either a certificate of plan approval issued by ABS, or written statements signed by the designer and builder which confirm that they have respectively designed and built the yacht in accordance with the ABS Guide.	MoMu0,1,2
3.03.2	Any significant repairs or modifications to the hull, deck, coachroof, keel or appendages, on a yacht defined in table 2 shall be certified by one of the methods above and an appropriate written statement or statements shall be on board.	MoMu0,1,2
3.04	**Stability - Monohulls**	
3.04.1	Either with, or without, reasonable intervention from the crew a yacht shall be capable of self-righting from an inverted position. Self-righting shall be achievable whether or not the rig is intact.	Mo0
3.04.2	A yacht shall be designed and built to resist capsize.	Mo0,1,2,3,4
3.04.3	*A National Authority or race organizer should require compliance with a minimum stability or stability/buoyancy index. Attention is drawn to the stability index in IMS Regulation 201.*	Mo0,1,2,3,4
3.04.4	*ISO 12217-2 may be used as a guide to general suitability for competition in Special Regulations race categories as follows:*	Mo0,1,2,3,4

Table 3

ISO Category	A	B	C	Mo0,1,2,3,4
SR Category	1-2	3	4	Mo0,1,2,3,4
Use of the ISO or any other index does not guarantee total safety or total freedom of risk from capsize or sinking.				Mo0,1,2,3,4

ISAF Special Regulations Governing Offshore and Oceanic Equipment and Preparation
Including US SAILING Prescriptions

		Category
3.05	**Stability and Flotation - Multihulls** *Attention is drawn to ISO 12217-2.*	
3.05.1	Adequate watertight bulkheads and compartments (which may include permanently installed flotation material) in each hull shall be provided to ensure that a multihull is effectively unsinkable and capable of floating in a stable position with at least half the length of one hull flooded. (see 3.13).	Mo0,1,2,3,4
3.05.2	Multihulls built on or after 1/99 shall in every hull without accommodation be divided at intervals of not more than 4m (13ft 3") by one or more transverse watertight bulkheads.	Mo0,1,2,3,4
3.06	**Exits - Monohulls**	

Table 4

LOA	Earliest of Age or Series Date	Detail	Mo0,1,2,3,4
8.5 m (28 ft) and over	1/95 and after	Yachts shall have at least two exits. At least one exit shall be located forward of the foremost mast except where structural features prevent its installation.	

3.07	**Exits - Multihulls**	Mo0,1,2,3,4
3.07.1	Each hull which contains accommodation shall have at least two exits	Mo0,1,2,3,4
3.07.2	In multihulls of 12m (39.4ft) LOA and greater each hull which contains accommodation shall have:-	Mo0,1,2,3,4
a)	an escape hatch for access to and from the hull in the event of an inversion	Mo0,1,2,3,4
b)	*The recommended minimum clearance diameter through a multihull escape hatch is 450mm or when the escape hatch is not circular, sufficient clearance to allow a crew member to pass through fully clothed.*	Mo0,1,2,3,4
c)	In a multihull first launched on or after 1/03 each escape hatch shall comply with 3.07.2(b) above.	Mo0,1,2,3,4
d)	When the yacht is inverted each escape hatch shall be above the waterline	Mo0,1,2,3,4
e)	In a multihull first launched on or after 1/01 each escape hatch shall be at or near the midships station	Mo0,1,2,3,4
f)	In a catamaran first launched on or after 1/03 each escape hatch shall be on the inner side of each hull	Mo0,1,2,3,4
g)	A catamaran first launched on or after 1/03 with a central nacelle shall have on the underside of the yacht around the central nacelle, handholds of sufficient capacity to enable all persons on board to hold on and/or clip on securely.	Mo0,1,2,3,4

ISAF Special Regulations Governing Offshore and Oceanic Equipment and Preparation
Including US SAILING Prescriptions

		Category
h)	*It is recommended that in a catamaran with a central nacelle, each hull should have an emergency refuge, accessible via a special hatch in the side of the hull nearest the central nacelle, which hatch may be opened and closed from the inside and outside.*	Mo0,1,2,3,4
i)	A trimaran of 12m (39.4ft) LOA first launched on or after 1/03 shall have at least two escape hatches in accordance with 3.07.2 (b)	Mo0,1,2,3,4
j)	A trimaran shall have on the underside of the yacht around the central hull, handholds of sufficient capacity to enable all persons on board to hold on and/or clip on securely.	Mo0,1,2,3,4
k)	Each escape hatch must have been opened both from inside and outside within 6 months prior to an intended race.	Mo0,1,2,3,4
3.07.3	Multihulls of less than 12m (39.4ft) LOA shall comply either with 3.07.2 or with the following:-	Mu2,3,4
a)	each hull which contains accommodation shall have, for the purpose of cutting an escape hatch, appropriate tools kept ready for instant use adjacent to the intended cutting site. Each tool shall be secured to the vessel by a line and a clip, and	Mu2,3,4
b)	in each hull at a station where an emergency hatch may be cut, the cutting line shall be clearly marked both inside and outside with an outline and the words "ESCAPE CUT HERE".	Mu2,3,4

3.08	Hatches & Companionways	
3.08.1	No hatch forward of the maximum beam station shall open in such a way that the lid or cover moves into the open position towards the inside of the hull (excepting ports having an area of less than 0.071m2 (110 sq in)).	**
3.08.2	A hatch shall be:	
a)	so arranged as to be above the water when the hull is heeled 90 degrees	**
b)	permanently attached	**
c)	capable of being firmly shut immediately and remaining firmly shut in a 180 degree capsize (inversion)	**
3.08.3	A companionway hatch extending below the local sheerline, shall:	
a)	not be permitted in a yacht with a cockpit opening aft to the sea (3.09.6)	**
b)	be capable of being blocked off up to the level of the local sheerline, provided that the companionway hatch shall continue to give access to the interior with the blocking devices (e.g. washboards) in place.	**

ISAF Special Regulations Governing Offshore and Oceanic Equipment and Preparation
Including US SAILING Prescriptions

		Category
3.08.4	A companionway hatch shall:	
a)	be fitted with a strong securing arrangement which shall be operable from the exterior and interior including when the yacht is inverted.	**
b)	have any blocking devices	**
i	capable of being retained in position with the hatch open or shut	**
ii	whether or not in position in the hatchway, secured to the yacht (e.g. by lanyard) for the duration of the race, to prevent their being lost overboard	**
iii	permit exit in the event of inversion	**

3.09 Cockpits - Attention is drawn to ISO 11812

3.09.1	cockpits shall be structurally strong, self-draining quickly by gravity at all angles of heel and permanently incorporated as an integral part of the hull.	**
3.09.2	cockpits must be essentially watertight, that is, all openings to the hull must be capable of being strongly and rigidly secured	**
3.09.3	a bilge pump outlet pipe or pipes shall not be connected to a cockpit drain . See 3.09.8 for cockpit drain minimum sizes.	**
3.09.4	A cockpit sole shall be at least 2% LWL above LWL (or in IMS yachts first launched before 1/03, at least 2% L above LWL)	**
3.09.5	a bow, lateral, central or stern well shall be considered a cockpit for the purposes of 3.09	**
3.09.6	In cockpits opening aft to the sea structural openings aft shall be not less in area than 50% maximum cockpit depth x maximum cockpit width.	**
3.09.7	**Cockpit volume**	

Table 5

earliest of age or series date	detail	Race Category
before 4/92	the total volume of all cockpits below lowest coamings shall not exceed 6% (LWL x maximum beam x freeboard abreast the cockpit).	MoMu0,1
before 4/92	he total volume of all cockpits below lowest coamings shall not exceed 9% (LWL x maximum beam x freeboard abreast the cockpit).	MoMu0,1
4/92 and after	as above for the appropriate category except that "lowest coamings" shall not include any aft of the FA station and no extension of a cockpit aft of the working deck shall be included in calculation of cockpit volume	**
Note	*IMS-rated boats may use instead of LWL, maximum beam, freeboard abreast the cockpit, the IMS terms L, B and FA.*	**

ISAF Special Regulations Governing Offshore and Oceanic Equipment and Preparation
Including US SAILING Prescriptions

		Category
3.09.8	**Cockpit drains**	
	See 3.09.1. Cockpit drain cross section area (after allowance for screens if fitted) shall be:-	
a)	in yachts with earliest of age or series date before 1/72 or in any yacht under 8.5m (28ft) LOA - at least that of 2 x 25mm (one inch) unobstructed openings or equivalent	**
b)	in yachts with earliest of age or series date 1/72 and later - at least that of 4 x 20mm (3/4 inch) unobstructed openings or equivalent	**
	US SAILING prescribes that cockpit drains shall be accessible for cleaning	**
3.10	**Sea cocks or valves**	
	Sea cocks or valves shall be permanently installed on all through-hull openings below LWL except integral deck scuppers, shaft log, speed indicators, depth finders and the like, however a means of closing such openings shall be provided.	**
3.11	**Sheet winches.**	
	Sheet winches shall be mounted in such a way that an operator is not required to be substantially below deck.	**
3.12	**Mast step.**	
	The heel of a keel stepped mast shall be securely fastened to the mast step or adjoining structure.	**
3.13	**Watertight Bulkheads**	
	Multihulls see also 3.05	
3.13.1	A hull shall have either a watertight "crash" bulkhead within 15% of LOA from the bow and abaft the forward end of LWL, or permanently installed closed-cell foam buoyancy effectively filling the forward 30% LOA of the hull.	Mo0Mu0,1, 2,3,4
3.13.2	Any required watertight bulkhead shall be strongly built to take a full head of water pressure without allowing any leakage into the adjacent compartment.	Mo0Mu0,1, 2,3,4
3.13.3	A yacht shall have at least two watertight transverse main bulkheads (in additition to "crash" bulkheads at bow or stern)	Mo0
3.13.4	Outside deck access for inspection and pumping shall be provided to every watertight compartment terminated by a hull section bulkhead, except that deck access to extreme end "crash" compartments is not required.	Mo0
3.13.5	An access hatch shall be provided in every required watertight bulkhead (except a "crash" bulkhead). In yachts first launched 1/03 and after, every access hatch shall have closures permanently attached.	Mo0
a)	*An access hatch in a watertight bulkhead should have closures permanently attached*	Mo0

US Edition 2004 - 2005

ISAF Special Regulations Governing Offshore and Oceanic Equipment and Preparation
Including US SAILING Prescriptions

		Category
b)	*An access hatch should be capable of being securely shut within 5 seconds*	Mo0
3.13.6	*It is strongly recommended that*	Mo0
a)	*an extreme end "crash" bulkhead should be provided at the stern. If practicable the aft "crash" bulkhead should be forward of the rudder post.*	Mo0
b)	*after flooding any one major compartment, a yacht should be capable of providing shelter and sustenance for a full crew for 1 week in another, dry compartment having direct access to the deck*	Mo0
c)	*compartments between watertight bulkheads should be provided with a means of manually pumping out from a position outside the compartment*	Mo0
3.14	**Pulpits, stanchions, lifelines - Attention is drawn to ISO 15085**	
3.14.1	When due to the particular design of a multihull it is impractical to precisely follow Special Regulations regarding pulpits, stanchions, lifelines, the regulations for monohulls shall be followed as closely as possible with the aim of minimizing the risk of people falling overboard.	Mu0,1,2,3,4
	US SAILING prescribes that all crew working areas shall be protected by lifelines or jackstays and safety harness attachment points. Lifelines or jackstays with or without safety harness attachment points may be substituted for pulpits.	Mu0,1,2,3,4
3.14.2	Lifelines required in Special Regulations shall be "taut".	**
a)	*As a guide, when a deflecting force of 50 N (5.1 kgf, 11.2 lbf) is applied to a lifeline midway between supports, the lifeline should not deflect more than 50 mm.*	**
3.14.3	The following shall be provided:	**
a)	*a bow pulpit forward of the headstay (however on yachts under 8.5 m (28 ft) the bow pulpit may be aft of the headstay provided the forward upper rail is within 405 mm (16 in) of the headstay) with vertical height and openings essentially conforming to Table 7. Bow pulpits may be open but the opening between the pulpit and any part of the boat shall never be greater than 360mm (14.2") (this requirement shall be checked by presenting a 360mm (14.2") circle inside the opening)*	Mo0Mu0,1, 2,3,4
b)	*a stern pulpit, or lifelines arranged as an adequate substitute, with vertical openings conforming to Table 7*	Mo0Mu0,1, 2,3,4
c)	lifelines (guardlines) supported on stanchions, which, with pulpits, shall form an effectively continuous barrier around a working deck for man-overboard prevention. Lifelines shall be permanently supported at intervals of not more than 2.20m (86.6") and shall not pass outboard of supporting stanchions	**

ISAF Special Regulations Governing Offshore and Oceanic Equipment and Preparation
Including US SAILING Prescriptions

		Category
d)	upper rails of pulpits at no less height above the working deck than the upper lifelines as in Table 7.	**
e)	Openable upper rails in bow pulpits shall be secured shut whilst racing	**
f)	Pulpits and stanchions shall be permanently installed. When there are sockets or studs, these shall be through-bolted, bonded or welded. The pulpit(s) and/or stanchions fitted to these shall be mechanically retained without the help of the life-lines. Without sockets or studs, pulpits and/or stanchions shall be through- bolted, bonded or welded.	**
g)	The bases of pulpits and stanchions shall not be further inboard from the edge of the appropriate working deck than 5% of maximum beam or 150 mm (6 in), whichever is greater.	**
h)	Stanchion bases shall not be situated outboard of a working deck. For the purpose of this rule a stanchion or pulpit base shall be taken to include a sleeve or socket into which a stanchion or pulpit tube is fitted but shall exclude a baseplate which carries fixings into the deck or hull.	**
i)	Provided the complete lifeline enclosure is supported by stanchions and pulpit bases effectively within the working deck, lifeline terminals and support struts may be fixed to a hull aft of the working deck	**
j)	Lifelines need not be fixed to a bow pulpit if they terminate at, or pass through, adequately braced stanchions set inside and overlapping the bow pulpit, provided that the gap between the upper lifeline and the bow pulpit does not exceed 150 mm (6 in).	**
k)	Stanchions shall be straight and vertical except that:-	**
i)	within the first 50 mm (2 in) from the deck, stanchions shall not be displaced horizontally from the point at which they emerge from the deck or stanchion base by more than 10 mm (3/8 in),and	**
ii)	stanchions may be angled to not more than 10 degrees from vertical at any point above 50 mm (2 in) from the deck.	**
3.14.4	**Special requirements for pulpits, stanchions, lifelines on multihulls**	
a)	on a trimaran - a bow pulpit on the main hull, with lifelines around the main hull supported on stanchions. The lifelines may be interrupted where there are nets or crossbeam wings outboard of the main hull	Mu0,1,2,3,4
b)	on a trimaran - where a net joins the base of a bow pulpit on the main hull, an additional lifeline from the top of the pulpit to the forward crossbeam at or outboard of the crossbeam mid-point.	Mu0,1,2,3,4

US Edition 2004 - 2005

ISAF Special Regulations Governing Offshore and Oceanic Equipment and Preparation
Including US SAILING Prescriptions

		Category
c)	on a trimaran - at a main or emergency steering position on an outrigger with or without a cockpit, lifelines protecting an arc of 3 meters diameter centered on the steering position. (When measuring between lifelines their taut, unreflected positions shall be taken for this purpose).	Mu0,1,2,3,4
d)	on a catamaran - lifelines from bow to stern on each hull. A catamaran without a forward or aft crossbeam shall have transverse lifelines at the extremity of the net forward and aft. The transverse lifelines shall be attached to bow and stern pulpits or superstructure. A webbing, strop or rope (minimum diameter 6mm) shall be rove zig-zag between the transverse lifelines and the net.	Mu0,1,2,3,4
3.14.5	Lifeline height, vertical openings, number of lifelines	**

Table 7

LOA	earliest of age/series date	minimum requirements
under 8.5 m(28 ft)	before1/92	taut single lifeline at a height of no less than 450 mm (18 in) above the working deck. No vertical opening shall exceed 560 mm (22 in).
under 8.5 m(28 ft)	1/92 and after	as for under 8.5 m(28 ft) in table 7 above, except that when an intermediate lifeline is fitted no vertical opening shall exceed 380 mm (15 in).
8.5 m (28 ft) and over	before1/93	taut double lifeline with upper lifeline at a height of no less than 600 mm (24 in) above the working deck. No vertical opening shall exceed 560 mm (22 in)
8.5 m (28 ft)and over	1/93 and after	as 8.5 m (28 ft) and over in Table 7 above, except that no vertical opening shall exceed 380 mm (15 in).
all	all	on yachts with intermediate lifelines the intermediate line shall be not less than 230 mm (9 in) above the working deck *and shall be of the same construction and general arrangements as required for the upper.*

3.14.6	Lifeline minimum diameters, required materials, specifications	
a)	*All* Lifelines shall be stranded stainless steel wire of minimum diameter in table 8 below. Lifelines installed from 1/99 shall be uncoated and used without close-fitting sleeving.	**
	Notwithstanding 3.14.6 (a) above, temporary sleeving may be fitted provided it is regularly removed for inspection.	**
b)	Grade 316 stainless wire is recommended.	**
c)	A taut lanyard of synthetic rope may be used to secure lifelines provided the gap it closes does not exceed 100 mm (4 in).	**

21

		Category
d)	All wire, fittings, anchorage points, fixtures and lanyards shall comprise a lifeline enclosure system which has at all points at least the breaking strength of the required lifeline wire.	**

Table 8

LOA	minimum wire diameter
under 8.5 m(28 ft)	3 mm (1/8 in)
8.5m - 13 m	4 mm (5/32 in)
over 13 m (43 ft)	5 mm (3/16 in)

3.14.7	Pulpits, stanchions, lifelines - limitations on materials	**

Table 9

Earliest of Age or Series Date	detail
before 1/87	carbon fibre is not recommended in stanchions pulpits and lifelines.
1/87 and after	stanchions, pulpits and lifelines shall not be made of carbon fibre.

3.15 Multihull Nets or Trampolines

3.15.1	The word "net" is interchangeable with the word "trampoline"	Mu0,1,2,3,4
a)	A net shall be:-	Mu0,1,2,3,4
b)	essentially horizontal	Mu0,1,2,3,4
c)	made from durable woven webbing, water permeable fabric, or mesh with openings not larger than 5.08cm (2 inches) in any dimension. Attachment points shall be planned to avoid chafe. The junction between a net and a yacht shall present no risk of foot trapping	Mu0,1,2,3,4
d)	solidly fixed at regular intervals on transverse and longitudinal support lines and shall be fine-stitched to a bolt rope	Mu0,1,2,3,4
e)	able to carry the full weight of the crew either in normal working conditions at sea or in case of capsize when the yacht is inverted.	Mu0,1,2,3,4
f)	*It is recommended that lines used to tie the nets should be individually tied and not continuously connected to more than four attachment points per connecting line.*	Mu0,1,2,3,4
3.15.2	**Trimarans with double crossbeams**	
a)	a trimaran with double crossbeams shall have nets on each side covering:-	
b)	the rectangles formed by the crossbeams, central hull and outriggers	Mu0,1,2,3,4

US Edition 2004 - 2005

ISAF Special Regulations Governing Offshore and Oceanic Equipment and Preparation
Including US SAILING Prescriptions

			Category
	c)	the triangles formed by the aft end of the central pulpit, the mid-point of each forward crossbeam, and the intersection of the crossbeam and the central hull	Mu0,1,2,3,4
	d)	the triangles formed by the aftermost part of the cockpit or steering position (whichever is furthest aft), the mid-point of each after crossbeam, and the intersection of the crossbeam and the central hull; except that:-	Mu0,1,2,3,4
	e)	the requirement in 3.15.2(d) shall not apply when cockpit coamings and/or lifelines are present which comply with the minimum height requirements in Table 7	Mu0,1,2,3,4
3.15.3		**Trimarans with single crossbeams**	
	a)	a trimaran with single crossbeams shall have nets between the central hull and each outrigger:-	Mu0,1,2,3,4
	b)	on each side between two straight lines from the intersection of the crossbeam and the outrigger, respectively to the aft end of the pulpit on the central hull, and to the aftermost point of the cockpit or steering position on the central hull (whichever is furthest aft)	Mu0,1,2,3,4
3.16		**Catamarans**	
	a)	On a catamaran the total net surface shall be limited:	
	b)	laterally by the hulls	Mu0,1,2,3,4
	c)	longitudinally by transverse stations through the forestay base, and the aftermost point of the boom lying fore and aft. However, a catamaran with a central nacelle (non-immersed) may satisfy the regulations for a trimaran	Mu0,1,2,3,4
3.17		**Toe Rail or Foot-stop**	
3.17.1		A toe rail of minimum height 25 mm (1 in) shall be permanently installed around the foredeck from abreast the mast, except in way of fittings and not further inboard from the edge of the working deck than one third of the local half-beam.	Mo0,1,2,3
3.17.2		The following variations shall apply:-	Mo0,1,2,3

Table 10

LOA	Earliest of Age or Series Date	minimum requirements	
any	before 1/81	a toe rail minimum height of 20 mm (3/4 in) is acceptable.	Mo0,1,2,3
any	before 1/93	an additional lifeline of minimum height 25 mm (1 in) and maximum height 50 mm (2 in) is acceptable in lieu of a toe rail (but shall not count as an intermediate lifeline).	Mo0,1,2,3
any	1/94 and after	the toe rail shall be fitted as close as practicable to the vertical axis of stanchion bases but not further inboard than 1/3 the local half-beam.	Mo0,1,2,3

ISAF Special Regulations Governing Offshore and Oceanic Equipment and Preparation
Including US SAILING Prescriptions

		Category
3.18	**Toilet**	
3.18.1	A toilet, permanently installed	MoMu0,1,2
3.18.2	A toilet, permanently installed or fitted bucket	MoMu3,4
3.19	**Bunks**	
3.19.1	Bunks, permanently installed, one for each member of the declared crew	MoMu0
3.19.2	Bunks, permanently installed	Mu0,1,2,3,4
3.20	**Cooking facilities**	
3.20.1	A cooking stove, permanently installed or securely fastened with safe accessible fuel shutoff control capable of being safely operated in a seaway.	MoMu0,1,2,3
3.21	**Drinking Water Tanks & Drinking Water**	
3.21.1	Tanks	MoMu0,1,2,3
a)	A yacht shall have a permanently installed delivery pump and water tank(s):	MoMu0,1,2,3
i	dividing the water supply into at least three compartments	MoMu0
ii	dividing the water supply into at least two compartments	MoMu1
3.21.2	Drinking Water	
a)	when not specified in the Notice of Race the quantity of drinking water on board at the start of a race shall be:	MoMu0
i	in the absence of a watermaker, at least 9 litres (2 UK gallons or 2.4 US gallons) per person per 1000 miles or	MoMu0
ii	when a watermaker is on board at least 3 litres (0.7 UK gallon or 0.8 US gallon) per person per 1000 miles.	MoMu0
3.21.3	Emergency water	
a)	at least 9 litres (2 UK gallons, 2.4 US gallons) of drinking water for emergency use shall be provided in a dedicated and sealed container or container(s)	MoMu0,1,2,3
3.22	**Hand holds.**	
	Adequate hand holds shall be fitted below deck so that crew members may move about safely at sea. *A hand hold should be capable of withstanding without rupture a side force of 1500N - attention is drawn to ISO 15085.*	**
3.23	**Bilge Pumps and Buckets**	
3.23.1	No bilge pump may discharge into a cockpit unless that cockpit opens aft to the sea.	**
3.23.2	Bilge pumps shall not be connected to cockpit drains. (3.09)	**
3.23.3	Bilge pumps and strum boxes shall be readily accessible for maintenance and for clearing out debris	**

ISAF Special Regulations Governing Offshore and Oceanic Equipment and Preparation
Including US SAILING Prescriptions

		Category
3.23.4	Unless permanently installed, each bilge pump handle shall be provided with a lanyard or catch or similar device to prevent accidental loss	**
3.23.5	The following shall be provided:	
a)	two permanently installed manual bilge pumps, one operable from above, the other from below deck. Each pump shall be operable with all cockpit seats, hatches and companionways shut and shall have permanently installed discharge pipe(s) of sufficient capacity to accommodate simultaneously both pumps	Mo0,1,2
b)	one permanently installed manual bilge pump either above or below deck. The pump shall be operable with all cockpit seats, hatches and companionways shut and shall have a permanently installed discharge pipe.	Mu0,1,2
c)	multihulls shall have provision to pump out all watertight compartments (except those filled with impermeable buoyancy).	Mu0,1,2,3,4
d)	one permanently installed manual bilge pump operable with all cockpit seats, hatches and companionways shut	Mo3
e)	one manual bilge pump	Mo4
f)	two buckets of stout construction each with at least 9 litres (2 UK gallons, 2.4 US gallons) capacity. Each bucket to have a lanyard.	**
3.24	**Compass**	
3.24.1	The following shall be provided:-	
a)	a marine magnetic compass, independent of any power supply, permanently installed and correctly adjusted with deviation card	**
b)	a compass which may be hand-held	MoMu0,1,2,3
3.25	**Halyards.**	
	No mast shall have less than two halyards, each capable of hoisting a sail.	**
	Boom Support. US SAILING prescribes that some means must exist to prevent the boom from dropping if support from the mainsail and/or halyard fails. Topping lifts or supporting vangs are acceptable for this purpose.	**
3.26	**Bow fairlead**	
	A bow fairlead, closed or closable and a cleat or securing arrangement, suitable for towing shall be permanently installed.	Mo0
3.27	**Navigation Lights (see 2.03.3)**	
3.27.1	Navigation lights shall be mounted so that they will not be masked by sails or the heeling of the yacht.	**
3.27.2	Navigation lights shall not be mounted below deck level and should be at no less height than immediately under the upper lifeline.	**

ISAF Special Regulations Governing Offshore and Oceanic Equipment and Preparation Including *US SAILING Prescriptions*

		Category
3.27.3	Navigation light intensity	**

Table 11

LOA	Guide to required minimum power rating for an electric bulb in a navigation light.
under 12 m (39.4 ft)	10 W
12 m (39.4 ft) and above	25 W

	Category
US SAILING prescribes that in the US compliance with the recommendations of COLREGS shall suffice in satisifying these regulation, COLREGS Requirements are as follows;	**

Table 14

LOA	Light	Luminous Intensity (candelas)	Minimum Range of visibility
under 39.4 ft	Side	0.9	1 mile
	Stern	4.3	2 miles
39.4 ft and above	Side	4.3	2 miles
and less than 164 ft	Stern	4.3	2 miles

3.27.4	reserve navigation lights shall be carried having the same minimum specifications as the navigation lights above, with a separable power source, and wiring or supply system essentially separate from that used for the normal navigation lights	MoMu0,1,2,3
3.27.5	spare bulbs for navigation lights shall be carried, or for lights not dependent on bulbs, appropriate spares.	**

3.28   Engines, generators, fuel

3.28.1	A securely covered inboard propulsion engine shall be provided together with permanently installed exhaust and fuel supply systems and fuel tank(s)	Mo0,1,2, Mu0
3.28.1.1	A propulsion engine shall be provided, either in accordance with 3.28.1 above, or as an outboard engine with associated tanks and fuel supply systems, all securely fastened.	Mo3
3.28.2	A propulsion engine shall be provided, either in accordance with 3.28.1 above or in a multihull of less than 12.0m (39.4ft) LOA an outboard engine together with permanently installed fuel supply systems and fuel tank(s).	Mu1,2,3
a)	A separate generator for electricity is optional. However, when a separate generator is carried it shall be permanently installed, securely covered, and shall have permanently installed exhaust and fuel supply systems and fuel tank(s). A separate generator shall comply with 3.28.3 (c) and (e)	MoMu0,1, 2,3
3.28.3	A propulsion engine required by Special Regulations shall:-	
a)	provide a minimum speed in knots of (1.8 x square root of LWL in metres) or (square root of LWL in feet)	MoMu0,1, 2,3

		Category
b)	have a minimum amount of fuel which may be specified in the Notice of Race but if not, shall be sufficient to be able to meet charging requirements for the duration of the race and to motor at the above minimum speed for at least 8 hours	MoMu0,1, 2,3
c)	have adequate protection from the effects of heavy weather	MoMu0,1, 2,3
d)	when an electric starter is the only method for starting the engine, have a separate battery, the primary purpose of which is to start the engine.	MoMu0,1, 2,3
e)	have each fuel tank provided with a shutoff valve. Except for permanently installed linings or liners, a flexible tank is not permitted as a fuel tank.	MoMu0,1, 2,3
3.28.4	*It is recommended that consideration be given to the installation of sealed batteries, noting however that special charging devices may be specified by the battery manufacturers.*	MoMu0,1, 2,3

3.29   Marine Radio, EPFS (Electronic Position-Fixing System)

		Category
	Provision of GMDSS and DSC is unlikely to be mandatory for small craft during the term of the present Special Regulations However it is recommended that owners consider including these facilities when installing new equipment.	MoMu0,1, 2,3
3.29.1	The following shall be provided:	MoMu0,1, 2,3
a)	A marine radio transceiver (or if stated in the Notice of Race, a satcom tranceiver). When the marine radio transceiver is VHF:	MoMu0,1, 2,3
i	it shall have a rated output power of 25W	MoMu0,1, 2,3
ii	it shall have a masthead antenna, and co-axial feeder cable with not more than 40% power loss	MoMu0,1, 2,3
iii	*The following types and lengths of co-axial feeder cable will meet the requirements of 3.29.1 (a)(ii): (lengths are given with approximate imperial equivalents) (a) up to 15m (50ft) - type RG8X ("mini 8"); (b) 15-28m (50-90ft) - type RG8U; (c) 28-43m (90-140ft) - type 9913F (uses conventional connectors, available from US supplier Belden); (d) 43-70m) 140-230ft - type LMR600 (uses special connectors, available from US supplier Times Microwave).*	MoMu0,1, 2,3
iv	*it should include channel 72 (an international ship-ship channel which, by common use, has become widely accepted as primary choice for ocean racing yachts anywhere in the world)*	MoMu0,1, 2,3
b)	An emergency antenna when the regular antenna depends upon the mast.	MoMu0,1, 2,3

US Edition 2004 - 2005

ISAF Special Regulations Governing Offshore and Oceanic Equipment and Preparation
Including US SAILING Prescriptions

		Category
c)	Independent of a main radio transceiver:-	
i	a watertight hand-held VHF transceiver	Mo0,1Mu 0,1,2,3,4
ii	the watertight hand-held marine VHF transceiver required in (I) above shall be stowed in accordance with 4.21.1	Mu3,4
iii	a radio receiver capable of receiving weather bulletins	**
d)	*it is strongly recommended that a hand-held watertight transceiver operating on one or more aviation frequencies including 121.5MHz should be provided. This will enable communications between the yacht and aircraft on SAR duties, not all of which have maritime VHF.*	
e)	a D/F (direction-finding) radio receiver working on eg 121.5MHz for man-overboard recovery (see 5.07)	MoMu0
f)	an EPFS (Electronic Position-Fixing System) (e.g. GPS)	MoMu0,1, 2,3

SECTION 4 - PORTABLE EQUIPMENT & SUPPLIES
for the yacht (for water & fuel see 3.21 and 3.28)

4.01	Sail Letters & Numbers	
4.01.1	Yachts which are not in an ISAF International Class or Recognized Class shall comply with RRS 77 and Appendix G as closely as possible, except that sail numbers allotted by a State authority are acceptable	**
4.01.2	Sail numbers and letters of the size carried on the mainsail must be displayed by alternative means when none of the numbered sails is set.	**
4.02	**Hull marking (colour blaze)**	
4.02.1	*To assist in SAR location a hull should show:*	
a)	*on the coachroof, deck and/or topsides where it can best be seen at least one block or strip of highly-visible colour (e.g. dayglo pink, orange or yellow) of at least one square meter in area*	MoMu0,1
b)	*on each underwater appendage an area of highly-visible colour.*	MoMu0,1
4.03	**Soft wood plugs**	
	Soft wood plugs, tapered and of the appropriate size, shall be attached or stowed adjacent to the appropriate fitting for every through-hull opening.	**

US Edition 2004 - 2005

ISAF Special Regulations Governing Offshore and Oceanic Equipment and Preparation
Including US SAILING Prescriptions

		Category
4.04	**Jackstays, Clipping Points and Static Safety Lines**	
4.04.1	The following shall be provided:	
a)	Jackstays:	MoMu0,1,2,3
i	attached to through-bolted or welded deck plates or other suitable and strong anchorage fitted on deck, port and starboard of the yacht's centre line to provide secure attachments for safety harness	MoMu0,1,2,3
ii	comprising stainless steel 1 x 19 wire of minimum diameter 5 mm (3/16 in), or webbing of equivalent strength *20kN (2,040 kgf or 4,500 lbf) min breaking strain webbing is recommended)*	MoMu0,1,2,3
	US SAILING prescribes that wire Jackstays may be of configurations other than 1 X 19.	MoMu0,1,2,3
iii	which, when made from stainless steel wire installed on or after 1/99 shall be uncoated and used without any sleeving	MoMu0,1,2,3
iv	*at least two of which should be fitted on the underside of a multihull in case of inversion.*	Mu0,1,2,3
4.04.2	**Clipping points:**	
a)	attached to through-bolted or welded deck plates or other suitable and strong anchorage points adjacent to stations such as the helm, sheet winches and masts, where crew members work for long periods.	MoMu0,1,2,3
b)	which, together with jackstays and static safety lines shall enable a crew member:	MoMu0,1,2,3
i	to clip on before coming on deck and unclip after going below	MoMu0,1,2,3
ii	whilst continuously clipped on, move readily between the working areas on deck and the cockpit(s) with the minimum of clipping and unclipping operations	MoMu0,1,2,3
c)	to enable two-thirds of the crew to be simultaneously clipped on without depending on jackstays	MoMu0,1,2,3
d)	in a trimaran with a rudder on the outrigger, adequate clipping points that are not part of the deck gear or the steering mechanism, in order that the steering mechanism can be reached by a crew member whilst clipped on.	Mu0,1,2,3
e)	*Warning - U-bolts as clipping points - see 5.02.1(a)*	
4.05	**Fire extinguishers**	
4.05.1	Fire extinguishers, at least two, readily accessible in suitable and different parts of the yacht	**

US Edition 2004 - 2005

ISAF Special Regulations Governing Offshore and Oceanic Equipment and Preparation
Including US SAILING Prescriptions

		Category
4.06	**Anchors**	
4.06.1	Anchors shall be carried according to the table below:	

Table 12

LOA	detail	Race Category
8.5 m (28 ft) and over	2 anchors together with a suitable combination of chain and rope, all ready for immediate use	MoMu0,1,2,3
under 8.5 m (28 ft)	1 anchor together with a suitable combination of chain and rope, all ready for immediate use	MoMu0,1,2,3
any	1 anchor, readily accessible	MoMu4

4.07	**Flashlight(s)**	
4.07.1	The following shall be provided:-	
a)	a watertight, high-powered flashlight or spotlight, with spare batteries and bulbs, and	MoMu0,1,2,3
b)	a watertight flashlight with spare batteries and bulb	**
c)	for Mu3,4 the watertight flashlight in 4.07.1 (b) shall be stowed in the grab bag	Mu3,4
4.08	**First Aid Manual and First Aid Kit**	
4.08.1	A suitable First Aid Manual shall be provided	**
	In the absence of a National Authority's requirement, the latest edition of one of the following is recommended:-	
a)	*International Medical Guide for Ships, World Health Organization, Geneva*	MoMu0,1
b)	*First Aid at Sea, by Douglas Justins and Colin Berry, published by Adlard Coles Nautical, London*	MoMu2,3,4
c)	*Le Guide de la medecine a distance, by Docteur J Y Chauve, published by Distance Assistance BP33 F-La Baule, cedex, France. An english translation may be available.*	**
	US SAILING endorses the above and additionally recommends the following manuals: Advanced First Aid by Peter Eastman, M.D., Cornell Maritime Press and Yachting First Aid by Drs. Bergman and Guzzeta (available from US SAILING)	**
4.08.2	A First Aid Kit shall be provided	**
4.08.3	*The contents and storage of the First Aid Kit should reflect the guidelines of the Manual carried, the likely conditions and duration of the passage, and the number of people aboard the yacht.*	**
4.08.4	*At least one member of the crew should be familiar with the management of medical emergencies that may occur at sea and radio communications operations for obtaining medical advice by radio (if carried) and (if carried) by Satcom. See 6.01*	**

US Edition 2004 - 2005

ISAF Special Regulations Governing Offshore and Oceanic Equipment and Preparation
Including US SAILING Prescriptions

		Category
4.09	**Foghorn**	
	A foghorn shall be provided	**
4.10	**Radar Reflector**	
4.10.1	A passive Radar Reflector (that is, a Radar Reflector without any power) shall be provided (see 4.10.3.3)	**
4.10.2	Attention is drawn to ISO8729. If a radar reflector is octahedral it must have a minimum diagonal measurement of 456 mm (18in), or if not octahedral must have a documented RCS (radar cross-section) of not less than 10 m2. The minimum effective height above water is 4.0 m (13 ft).	**
	US SAILING prescribes that in the US, radar reflectors shall have a minimum documented "equivalent echoing area" of 6 sq. m. Octahedral reflectors shall have a minimum diameter of 12 inches.	**
4.10.3.1	*The passive and active devices referred to in these notes and in 4.10.1 and 4.10.2 above are primarily intended for use in the X (9GHz) band*	**
4.10.3.2	*The most effective radar response from a yacht may be provided by an RTE (Radar Target Enhancer) which may be on board in addition to the required passive reflector. An RTE should conform to Recommendation ITU-R 1176. An RTE is strongly recommended.*	**
4.10.3.3	*The display of a passive reflector or the operation of an RTE is for the person in charge to decide according to prevailing conditions.*	**
4.10.3.4	*Attention is drawn to a new performance standard for radar reflectors in draft at IMO ref Nav 49/19 Annex 12 expected to be adopted during 2004 intended to ensure a better and more consistent level of performance than that achieved by ISO 8729 or a 456mm (18") octahedral reflector. A passive reflector conforming to the new standard may be in the form of a cylinder of not more than weight 5kg, height 750mm and diameter 300mm.*	**
4.10.3.5	*S (3GHz) band radar is often used by ships to complement X (9GHz) band radar. On S (3GHz) band a conventional reflector or RTE offers about 1/10 the response obtained on the X (9GHz) band.*	**
4.10.3.6	*Yachts are reminded that no reflector, active or passive, is a guarantee of detection or tracking by a vessel using radar.*	**
4.11	**Navigation Equipment**	
4.11.1	Charts	
	Navigational charts (not solely electronic), light list and chart plotting equipment shall be provided	**
4.11.2	Sextant	
	Navigators are recommended to carry a sextant with suitable tables and a timepiece as a backup navigation system.	MoMu0,1

		Category
4.12	**A durable stowage chart** A durable stowage chart shall be provided and shall be displayed in the main accommodation where it can best be seen, clearly marked with the location of the principal items of safety equipment.	**
4.13	**Echo sounder or lead line.** An echo sounder or lead line shall be provided	**
4.14	**Speedometer or distance measuring instrument (log).** A speedometer or distance measuring instrument (log) shall be provided	MoMu0,1, 2,3
4.15	**Emergency steering**	
4.15.1	Emergency steering shall be provided as follows:	
a)	except when the principal method of steering is by means of an unbreakable metal tiller, an emergency tiller capable of being fitted to the rudder stock	MoMu0,1, 2,3
b)	crews must be aware of alternative methods of steering the yacht in any sea condition in the event of rudder loss. At least one method must have been proven to work on board the yacht. An inspector may require that this method be demonstrated.	MoMu0,1, 2,3
4.16	**Tools and spare parts** Tools and spare parts, including effective means to quickly disconnect or sever the standing rigging from the hull shall be provided.	**
4.17	**Yacht's name** Yacht's name shall be on miscellaneous buoyant equipment, such as lifejackets, oars, cushions, lifebuoys and lifeslings etc.	**
4.18	**Marine grade retro-reflective material** Marine grade retro-reflective material shall be fitted to lifebuoys, lifeslings, liferafts and lifejackets. See Special Regulation 5.04, 5.08.	**
4.19	**EPIRBs**	
4.19.1	A 406 MHz EPIRB or an INMARSAT type "E" EPIRB shall be provided	MoMu0,1,2
4.19.2	*It is recommended that a 406 MHz EPIRB should include an internal GPS, and also a 121.5MHz transmitter for local homing. An INMARSAT Type "E" EPIRB includes both these devices.*	MoMu0,1,2
a)	A 406 MHz or Type "E" EPIRB shall be properly registered with the appropriate authority.	MoMu0,1,2
4.19.3	*Beacons with only 121.5MHz are no longer recommended for distress alerting. Satellite processing of 121.5 MHz is being phased out. 121.5MHz will continue to be used for local homing by on-board D/F systems and for local homing by SAR units.*	MoMu0,1,2
4.19.4	*EPIRBs should be tested in accordance with manufacturer's instructions when first commissioned and then at least annually.*	MoMu0,1,2

US Edition 2004 - 2005

ISAF Special Regulations Governing Offshore and Oceanic Equipment and Preparation
Including US SAILING Prescriptions

		Category
4.19.5	*A list of registration numbers of 406 EPIRBs should be maintained by event organizers and kept available for immediate use.*	MoMu0,1,2
4.19.6	*Consideration should be given to the provision of a locator device (eg an "Argos" beacon) operating on non-SAR frequencies, to aid salvage if a yacht is abandoned.*	MoMu0,1,2
	See 3.29.1(e) for on-board D/F and 5.07.1(b) for personal EPIRBs (PLBs)	MoMu0
	US SAILING requires the use of 406 EPIRBs (with or without GPS input), as USCG advises that rescue efforts will be launched immediately upon receipt of a distress signal from these units. Older units using 121.5 and 243.0 MHz may involve delays of several hours before search initiation, due to high false alarm rates for this equipment. USCG also advises that INMARSAT "E" Transmissions are not monitored by U.S. Rescue Coordination Centers and that slight delays are likely to occur while the commercial ground stations forward an alert to the USCG.	MoMu0,1,2
4.20	**LIFERAFTS**	
4.20.1	Liferaft Construction	
a)	Liferaft(s) shall be provided capable of carrying the whole crew and meeting the following requirements:-	MoMu0,1,2
b)	Liferaft(s) shall be built in accordance with SOLAS regulations (see the LSA code 1997 Chapter IV published by IMO) except that modifications in 4.20.1 (b)(I) and (b)(ii) below are acceptable	MoMu0
i	A liferaft which in all other respects is built to SOLAS regulations may however have a capacity of 4 persons or more (otherwise the smallest SOLAS liferaft is for 6 persons)	MoMu0
ii	A SOLAS liferaft may be stowed in a purpose-built compartment as in 4.20.2(b) in lieu of a conventional transportable rigid container	MoMu0
c)	Each liferaft shall contain at least a SOLAS "A" pack	MoMu0
d)	Liferaft(s) shall be either:-	MoMu1,2
i	in accordance with SOLAS (which may be varied by 4.20.1(b)(I) and (b)(ii)), and also (varying 4.20 (c)) with the option of a SOLAS "B" pack, or	MoMu1,2
ii	in accordance with Special Regulations Appendix A Part I or Part II (Appendix A Part I is for liferafts manufactured before 1/03 which still *(1/06 in the U.S.)* have a valid service life and Appendix A Part II is the required standard for all other non-SOLAS liferafts)	MoMu1,2
e)	*When ISO 9650 is published as an International Standard (not a draft) it will be considered for possible acceptance as an alternative to the ISAF Special Regulations Appendix A Part II specification.*	MoMu1,2

ISAF Special Regulations Governing Offshore and Oceanic Equipment and Preparation
Including US SAILING Prescriptions

		Category
	US SAILING recommends that liferafts be equipped with insulated floors for events that take place in waters of less than 68 deg F. (20 deg C)	MoMu1,2
	US SAILING prescribes that liferafts shall be equipped with canopies.	MoMu1,2
4.20.2	Liferaft Stowage	
	A Liferaft shall be stowed either:-	
a)	in a transportable rigid container on the working deck or in the cockpit, or	MoMu1,2
b)	in a purpose-built rigid compartment opening into or adjacent to the cockpit or working deck, or opening through a transom, containing liferaft(s) only, provided that:	MoMu1,2
i	each compartment is watertight or self-draining (self-draining compartments will be counted as part of the cockpit volume except when entirely above working deck level or when draining independently overboard from a transom stowage); and	MoMu1,2
ii	the cover of each compartment is capable of being easily opened under water pressure; and	MoMu1,2
iii	the compartment is designed and built to allow the liferaft to be removed and launched quickly and easily; or	MoMu1,2
c)	(only available to yachts with age or series date before 6/01) packed in a valise not exceeding 40kg securely stowed below deck adjacent to the companionway	MoMu1,2
d)	A SOLAS liferaft may be stowed only in accordance with either 4.20.2 (a) or (b)	MoMu0,1,2
e)	*It is strongly recommended that*	
f)	*Liferaft stowage should follow 4.20.2(b) above; and*	MoMu,1,2
g)	*liferafts of more than 40kg weight should be stowed in such a way that they can be dragged or slid into the sea without significant lifting; and*	MoMu0,1,2
h)	*the yacht end of the painter should be permanently made fast to a strong point on board the yacht; and*	MoMu0,1,2
i)	*on a multihull, liferaft stowage should be such that the liferaft can be readily removed and launched regardless of whether or not the yacht is inverted.*	Mu0,1,2
4.20.3	Recovery Time.	
a)	Each raft shall be capable of being got to the lifelines or launched within 15 seconds.	MoMu0,1,2

ISAF Special Regulations Governing Offshore and Oceanic Equipment and Preparation
Including US SAILING Prescriptions

		Category
4.20.4	**Liferaft servicing and inspection**	
a)	Servicing and/or inspection certificates or copies shall be kept on board the yacht	MoMu0,1,2
b)	Every SOLAS liferaft shall have a valid annual certificate of new or serviced status from the liferaft manufacturer or the manufacturer's approved service station	MoMu0,1,2
c)	For liferafts built to Special Regulations Appendix A part I each liferaft shall either have a valid annual certificate of new or serviced status from the liferaft manufacturer or the manufacturer's approved service station, or when a manufacturer so specifies it shall annually be inspected (not necessarily unpacked) and the yacht provided with written confirmation by the manufacturer or the manufacturer's approved service station stating that the inspection was satisfactory.	MoMu1,2
d)	A liferaft built in accordance with Special Regulations Appendix A part II shall either have a valid annual certificate of new or serviced status from the liferaft manufacturer or the manufacturer's approved service station, or when the liferaft has been built to follow the option of an extended period between initial services the liferaft, provided the manufacturer so specifies, shall have its first service no longer than 3 years after commissioning and its second service no longer than 2 years after the first. Subsequent services shall be at intervals of not more than 12 months.	MoMu1,2
e)	*Notwithstanding the specified servicing periods it is strongly recommended that a liferaft should be carefully inspected externally at least annually and taken for servicing if there is any sign of damage or deterioration.*	
4.21	**Grab Bags**	
4.21.1	**Grab Bag or emergency container for multihulls without liferafts**	
a)	A multihull without a liferaft shall stow in a watertight compartment, or in a grab bag supplied with a lanyard and clip, accessible with the multihull upright or inverted, the following items:-	Mu3,4
b)	Note: it is not required to duplicate items below which are already required by Special Regulations to be on board - this regulation covers only the stowage of those items:-	Mu3,4
c)	a watertight hand-held marine VHF transceiver plus a spare set of batteries	Mu3,4
d)	a watertight flashlight with spare batteries and bulb	Mu3,4
e)	2 red parachute and 3 red hand flares	Mu3,4
f)	a watertight strobe light with spare batteries	Mu3,4
g)	a knife	Mu3,4

ISAF Special Regulations Governing Offshore and Oceanic Equipment and Preparation
Including US SAILING Prescriptions

		Category
4.21.2	**Grab Bag to accompany liferafts**	
a)	*A yacht with a liferaft is recommended to stow in a grab bag with a lanyard and clip, the following items:-*	MoMu0,1,2
b)	*Note: it is not required to duplicate items below which are already required by Special Regulations to be on board - this regulation covers only the stowage of those items:-*	MoMu0,1,2
c)	*a watertight hand-held marine VHF transceiver plus a spare set of batteries*	MoMu0,1,2
d)	*a watertight flashlight with spare batteries and bulb*	MoMu0,1,2
e)	*2 red parachute and 3 red hand flares and cyalume-type chemical light sticks*	MoMu0,1,2
f)	*watertight hand-held EPFS (Electronic Position-Fixing System) (eg GPS)*	MoMu0,1,2
g)	*an SART (Search and Rescue Transponder)*	MoMu0,1,2
h)	*dry suits or survival bags*	MoMu0,1,2
i)	*second sea anchor for the liferaft (not required if the liferaft has already a spare sea anchor in its pack) (recommended standard ISO 17339) with swivel and >30m line diameter >9.5 mm*	MoMu0,1,2
j)	*two safety tin openers*	MoMu0,1,2
k)	*406MHz or type "E" EPIRB registered to the yacht (see 4.19.2)*	MoMu0,1,2
l)	*first-aid kit*	MoMu0,1,2
m)	*water*	MoMu0,1,2
n)	*signaling mirror*	MoMu0,1,2
o)	*high-energy food*	MoMu0,1,2
p)	*nylon string, polythene bags, seasickness tablets*	MoMu0,1,2
q)	*watertight hand-held aviation VHF transceiver (if race area warrants)*	MoMu0,1,2
4.22	**Lifebuoys**	
4.22.1	The following shall be provided within ***easy*** reach of the helmsman and ready for instant use:	**
a)	a lifebuoy with a self-igniting light and a drogue or a Lifesling with a self-igniting light and without a drogue.	**
	For Categories 0,1,2,3, US SAILING prescribes that the lifebuoy in 4.22.1 a) above shall be a Lifesling (without a drogue), equipped with self-igniting light within easy reach of the helmsman and ready for instant use. (See Appendix D).	MoMu0,1, 2,3
	For Category 4, US SAILING prescribes that the lifebuoy must be inherently buoyant.	MoMu4
b)	in addition to a) above, one lifebuoy within ***easy*** reach of the helmsman and ready for instant use, equipped with:	MoMu0,1,2
i	a whistle, a drogue, a self-igniting light and	MoMu0,1,2

US Edition 2004 - 2005

ISAF Special Regulations Governing Offshore and Oceanic Equipment and Preparation
Including US SAILING Prescriptions

			Category
	ii	a pole and flag. The pole shall be either permanently extended or be capable of being fully automatically extended (not extendable by hand) in less than 20 seconds. It shall be attached to the lifebuoy with 3 m (10 ft) of floating line and is to be of a length and so ballasted that the flag will fly at least 1.8 m (6 ft) off the water.	MoMu0,1,2
4.22.2		When at least two lifebuoys (and/or Lifeslings) are carried, at least one of them shall depend entirely on permanent (eg foam) buoyancy.	MoMu0,1,2
4.22.3		Each inflatable lifebuoy and any automatic device (eg pole and flag extended by compressed gas) shall be tested and serviced at intervals in accordance with its manufacturer's instructions.	**
4.22.4		Each lifebuoy or lifesling shall be fitted with marine grade retro-reflective material (4.18).	**

4.23	Pyrotechnic signals	
4.23.1	Pyrotechnic signals shall be provided conforming to SOLAS LSA Code Chapter III Visual Signals and not older than the stamped expiry date (if any) or if no expiry date stamped , not older than 4 years.	**

				Category
Table 13				
red parachute flares LSA III 3.1	red hand flares LSA III 3.2	white hand flares*	orange smoke LSA III 3.3	Race Category
6	4	4	2	MoMu0,1
4	4	4	2	MoMu2,3
	4	4	2	Mo4
2	4	4	2	Mu4

Specifications of white flares (except colour and candela rating) should comply with the LSA Code Chapter III 3.2

4.24 Heaving Line

a)	A heaving line shall be provided 15 m - 25 m (50 ft - 75 ft) length readily accessible to cockpit.	**
b)	*The "throwing sock" type is recommended - see Appendix D*	**
	US SAILING prescribes that the heaving line be of 1/4 in. (6 mm) minimum diameter, floating, UV-inhibited and readily accessible to the cockpit	**

4.25 Cockpit Knife

A strong, sharp knife, sheathed and securely restrained shall be provided readily accessible from the deck or a cockpit.	**

4.26 Storm & Heavy Weather Sails

4.26.1	*design*	
a)	*It is strongly recommended that owners consult their designer and sailmaker to decide the most effective size for storm and heavy weather sails. The purpose of these sails is to provide safe propulsion for the yacht in severe weather -they are not intended as part of the racing inventory. The areas below are maxima. Smaller areas are likely to suit some yachts according to their stability and other characteristics.*	**
4.26.2	*high visibility*	
a)	*It is strongly recommended that every storm sail should either be of highly-visible coloured material (eg dayglo pink, orange or yellow) or have a highly-visible coloured patch added on each side; and also that a rotating wing mast used in lieu of a trysail should have a highly-visible coloured patch on each side.*	**

ISAF Special Regulations Governing Offshore and Oceanic Equipment and Preparation
Including US SAILING Prescriptions

		Category
4.26.3	Materials	
a)	Aromatic polyamides, carbon and similar fibres shall not be used in a trysail or storm jib but spectra/dyneema and similar materials are permitted.	**
b)	*It is strongly recommended that a heavy-weather jib does not contain aromatic polyamides, carbon and similar fibres other than spectra/dyneema.*	**
4.26.4	The following shall be provided:-	
a)	sheeting positions on deck for each storm and heavy-weather sail;	**
b)	each storm or heavy-weather jib shall have a means to attach the luff to the stay, independent of any luff-groove device	**
c)	a storm trysail capable of being **attached to the mast and** sheeted independently of the boom with area not greater than 17.5% mainsail luff length x mainsail foot length. The storm trysail shall have neither headboard nor battens, however a storm trysail is not required in a yacht with a rotating wing mast which can adequately substitute for a trysail;	MoMu0,1,2
d)	the yacht's sail number and letter(s) placed on both sides of the trysail (or on a rotating wing mast as substitute for a trysail) in as large a size as practicable;	MoMu0,1,2
e)	a storm jib of area not greater than 5% height of the foretriangle squared, with luff maximum length 65% height of the foretriangle;	MoMu0,1,2
f)	*in addition to the storm jib required by 4.26.4 e)*, a heavy-weather jib (or heavy-weather sail in a yacht with no forestay) of area not greater than 13.5% height of the foretriangle squared and without reef points;	**
g)	and either a storm trysail as above, or mainsail reefing to reduce the luff by at least 40%.	MoMu3,4 *Mu2*
h)	In a yacht with an in-mast furling mainsail, the storm trysail must be capable of being set while the mainsail is furled.	MoMu0,1,2
i)	*A trysail track should allow for the trysail to be hoisted quickly when the mainsail is lowered whether or not the mainsail is stowed on the main boom.*	MoMu0,1,2
	In addition, US SAILING prescribes mainsail reefing to reduce the luff by at least 10% for sails built after 1 January 1997.	MoMu0,1, 2,3
4.27	**Drogue, Sea Anchor**	
	A drogue (for deployment over the stern), or alternatively a sea anchor or parachute anchor (for deployment over the bow), is strongly recommended (see Appendix F).	MoMu0,1

US Edition 2004 - 2005

ISAF Special Regulations Governing Offshore and Oceanic Equipment and Preparation
Including US SAILING Prescriptions

SECTION 5 - PERSONAL EQUIPMENT

		Category
5.01	**Lifejacket**	
5.01.1	Each crew member shall have a lifejacket as follows:-	**
a)	equipped with a whistle	**
b)	fitted with marine grade retro-reflective material (4.18)	**
c)	compatible with the wearer's safety harness	**
d)	if inflatable, regularly checked for air retention	**
e)	clearly marked with the yacht's or wearer's name	**
5.01.2	*It is strongly recommended that a lifejacket:-*	**
a)	*has a lifejacket light in accordance with SOLAS LSA code 2.2.3 (white, >0.75 candelas, >8 hours)*	**
b)	*has at least 150N buoyancy, arranged to securely suspend an unconscious man face upwards at approximately 45 degrees to the water surface- in accordance with EN396 or near equivalent*	**
c)	*has a crotch strap or thigh straps*	**
d)	*has a splashguard. See EN394*	**
e)	*if inflatable, has a compressed gas inflation system*	**
	US SAILING prescribes for categories 0, 1, 2, 3 either a Type 1 U.S. Coast Guard approved personal floatation device or an inflatable personal floatation device meeting the definition in the above paragraph and manufactured to either British national or European Community standards. A light should be fitted and a crotch strap is recommended on each lifejacket. Each inflatable device should be inflated and inspected annually. Service dates shall be marked on the floatation devices. This inflatable device may be integrated with a safety harness (see 5.02)	MoMu0,1, 2,3
	US SAILING prescribes for Category 4 lifejackets as above or U.S. Coast Guard approved Type III personal floatation devices.	MoMu4
	US SAILING prescribes that all personnel on deck shall wear personal floatation while starting and finishing without exception, and at all other times except when the Captain of the boat directs that it may be set aside.	**
	US SAILING note: As is true of all of these regulations, the prescriptions above do not necessarily replace the requirements of other governing authorities.	**

		Category
5.02	**Safety Harness and Safety Lines (tethers)**	
5.02.1	Each crew member shall have a harness, and a safety line not more than 2m long with a snaphook at each end.	MoMu0,1,2,3
a)	*Warning it is possible for a plain snaphook to disengage from a U-bolt if the hook is rotated under load at right-angles to the axis of the U-bolt. For this reason the use of snaphooks with positive locking devices is strongly recommended.*	MoMu0,1,2,3
5.02.2	At least 30% of the crew shall each, in addition to the above be provided with either:-	MoMu0,1,2,3
a)	a safety line not more than 1m long, or	MoMu0,1,2,3
b)	a mid-point snaphook on a 2m safety line	MoMu0,1,2,3
5.02.3	A safety line purchased in 1/01 or later shall have a coloured flag embedded in the stitching, to indicate an overload. A line which has been overloaded shall be replaced as a matter of urgency.	MoMu0,1,2,3
5.02.4	A crew member's lifejacket and harness shall be compatible	MoMu0,1,2,3
5.02.5	*It is strongly recommended that:-*	MoMu0,1,2,3
a)	*a harness and safety line should comply with EN 1095 (ISO 12401) or near equivalent*	MoMu0,1,2,3
b)	*static safety lines should be securely fastened at work stations*	MoMu0,1,2,3
c)	*a harness should be fitted with a crotch strap or thigh straps*	MoMu0,1,2,3
d)	*to draw attention to wear and damage, stitching on harness and safety lines should be of a colour contrasting strongly with the surrounding material*	MoMu0,1,2,3
e)	*snaphooks should be of a type which will not self-release from a U-bolt (5.02.1(a)) and which can be easily released under load (crew members are reminded that a personal knife may free them from a safety line in emergency)*	MoMu0,1,2,3
f)	*a crew member before a race should adjust a harness to fit then retain that harness for the duration of the race*	MoMu0,1,2,3
	US SAILING prescribes that the safety harness may be integrated with an inflatable personal floatation device (see 5.01) and recommends that such devices be employed whenever conditions warrant, and always in rough weather, on cold water, or at night, or under conditions of reduced visibility or when sailing short-handed.	MoMu0,1,2,3
	US SAILING prescribes that safety harnesses and PFD's shall be worn on category 0 and 1 races from sundown to sun up while on deck.	MoMu0,1
5.03	**Personal location lights**	
a)	Two packs of miniflares or two personal location lights (either SOLAS or strobe) shall be provided for each crew member: one should be attached to, or carried on, the person when on deck at night.	MoMu0

		Category
5.04	**Foul weather suits**	
a)	A foul weather suit with hood shall be supplied to each crew member.	MoMu0
b)	It is recommended that a foul weather suit should be fitted with marine-grade retro-reflective material, and should have high-visibility colours on its upper parts and sleeve cuffs. See 4.18	**
5.05	**Knife**	
	A knife, one shall be supplied to each crew member.	MoMu0
5.06	**Watertight flashlight**	
	A watertight flashlight, one shall be supplied to each crew member.	MoMu0
5.07	**Survival Equipment**	
5.07.1	One set of Survival Equipment shall be supplied to each crew member to include:	MoMu0
a)	an immersion suit (attention is drawn to pr EN1913-1 constant wear suits, and pr EN 1913-2 abandonment suits and the LSA Code Chapter II, 2,3).	MoMu0
b)	a suitable EPIRB or PLB (Personal Locator Beacon) capable of working with the on-board D/F receiver required in 3.29.1 (e)	MoMu0
c)	*It is strongly recommended that an immersion suit should be suplied to each crew member in a multihull in conditions where there is a potential for hypothermia*	Mu1,2,3,4
	US SAILING prescribes that an immersion suit as specified above for each crew member is strongly recommended above latitude 30.	Mu1,2
5.08	**Annual Man-Overboard Practice**	
	US SAILING prescribes that the "Quick-Stop" man-overboard procedure shall be practiced aboard the yacht at least once annually. A certificate of such practice shall be signed by participating crew members and kept aboard the yacht.	**
5.09	**CPR Training**	
	US SAILING recommends that at least two members of the crew be currently certified in cardiopulmonary resuscitation.	**
5.10	**Preventer or Boom Restraining Device**	
	US SAILING recommends that a preventer or boom restraining device should be rigged in such a manner that attachment can be easily and quickly made, with the boom fully extended (running) without leaving the deck or leaning overboard. A process and plan for its use should be part of the crew's training and practice. Recommended for all boats in all categories.	**

ISAF Special Regulations Governing Offshore and Oceanic Equipment and Preparation
Including US SAILING Prescriptions

SECTION 6 - TRAINING

		Category
6.01	**At least 30% of a crew including the skipper shall have undertaken training within the five years before the start of the race in both 6.02 topics for theoretical sessions, and 6.03 topics which include practical, hands-on sessions.**	MoMu0,1
6.01.1	*It is strongly recommended that all crew members should undertake personal survival training at least once every five years*	**
6.01.2	Except as otherwise provided in the Notice of Race, an in-date certificate gained at an ISAF Approved Offshore Personal Survival Training course shall be accepted by a race organizing authority as evidence of compliance with Special Regulation 6.01. See Appendix G - Model Training Course, for further details.	MoMu0,1
6.02	**Training topics for theoretical sessions**	
6.02.1	care and maintenance of safety equipment	MoMu0,1
6.02.2	storm sails	MoMu0,1
6.02.3	damage control and repair	MoMu0,1
6.02.4	heavy weather - crew routines, boat handling, drogues	MoMu0,1
6.02.5	man overboard prevention and recovery	MoMu0,1
6.02.6	giving assistance to other craft	MoMu0,1
6.02.7	hypothermia	MoMu0,1
6.02.8	SAR organization and methods	MoMu0,1
6.02.9	weather forecasting	MoMu0,1
	US SAILING prescribes that training under this Regulation shall take place in a program that is approved by US SAILING and that shall require a minimum of 8 hours. Competitors who are members of other National Governing Bodies may demonstrate that they have completed such training in accordance with the requirements of those organizations.	MoMu0,1

		Category
6.03	**Training topics for practical, hands-on sessions**	
6.03.1	liferafts and lifejackets	MoMu0,1
6.03.2	fire precautions and use of fire extinguishers	MoMu0,1
6.03.3	cpr and first aid	MoMu0,1
6.03.4	communications equipment (VHF, GMDSS, satcomms, etc.)	MoMu0,1
6.03.5	pyrotechnics and EPIRBs	MoMu0,1
6.04	**Routine training on board**	
6.04.1	*it is recommended that crews should practice safety routines at reasonable intervals including the drill for man-overboard recovery*	**
	US SAILING prescribes that each skipper in a category 0 or 1 race shall ensure that a minimum of 30 percent of the crew have been trained in the use of the boat's equipment, including: liferafts and lifejackets; communications; pyrotechnics; EPIRBs; and fire prevention and fire fighting. A record of this training shall be kept aboard the boat in a manner similar to that required for certifying man-overboard training.	MoMu0,1

APPENDIX A part I
Minimum Specifications for Yachtsmen's Liferafts
for liferafts manufactured prior to 1/03 *(At least 1/06 in the U.S.)*
Appendix A does not cover liferafts intended for category 0 races

1.0   General design

Liferaft(s) capable of carrying the whole crew shall meet the following requirements:

a)   Stowage - see Special Regulation 4.20.2

b)   Must be designed and used solely for saving life at sea

c)   The liferaft shall be so constructed that, when fully inflated and floating with the cover uppermost, it shall be stable in a seaway

d)   The construction of the liferaft shall include a canopy or cover, which shall unless when specified by the national Authority or Notice of Race automatically be set in place when the liferaft is inflated. This cover shall be capable of protecting the occupants against injury from exposure, and means shall be provided for collecting rain. The cover of the liferaft shall be of a highly visible colour.

e)   The liferaft shall be fitted with a painter line and shall have a lifeline becketed round the outside. A lifeline shall also be fitted round the inside of the liferaft

f)   The liferaft shall be capable of being readily righted by one person if it inflates in an inverted position

g)   The liferaft shall be fitted at each opening with efficient means to enable persons in the water to climb on board

h)   The liferaft shall be contained in a valise or other container so constructed as to be capable of withstanding hard wear under conditions met with at sea. The liferaft in its valise or other container shall be inherently buoyant

i)   The buoyancy of the liferaft shall be so arranged as to achieve a division into an even number of separate compartments, half of which shall be capable of supporting out of the water the number of persons which the liferaft is fit to accommodate, without reducing the total supporting area.

j)   The number of persons which an inflatable liferaft shall be permitted to accommodate shall be equal to:-

i   the greatest whole number obtained by dividing by .096 the volume, measured in cubic meters of the main buoyancy tubes (which for this purpose shall include neither the arches nor the thwarts if fitted) when inflated, or

ii   the greatest whole number obtained by dividing by 3720 the area measured in square centimeters of the floor (which for this purpose may include the thwart or thwarts if fitted) of the liferaft when inflated whichever number shall the the less

k)   The floor of the liferaft shall be waterproof and when specified by the National Authority or Notice of Race shall is strongly recommended to be capable of being sufficiently insulated against the cold either:-

i   by means of one or more compartments which the occupants can inflate if they so desire, or which inflate automatically and can be deflated and re-inflated by the occupants; or

ii   by other equally efficient means not dependent on inflation

2.0 Equipment

a)   one buoyant rescue quoit, attached to at least 30 meters of buoyant line

b)   one safety knife and one bailer

c)   two sponges

d)   one sea anchor or drogue permanently attached to the liferaft (the NMI pattern with anti-tangle lines compliance with ISO 17339 or equivalent is recommended)

e)   two paddles

f)   one repair outfit capable of repairing punctures in buoyancy compartments

g)   one topping-up pump or bellows

h)   one waterproof electric torch

i)   three hand-held red distress flare signals in accordance with SOLAS regulation 36

j)   six anti-seasickness tablets for each person which the liferaft is deemed fit to accommodate

k)   instructions on a plastic sheet on how to survive in the liferaft

l)   the liferaft shall be inflated by a gas which is not injurious to the occupants and the inflation shall take place automatically either on the pulling of a line or by some other equally simple and efficient method. Means shall be provided whereby a topping-up pump or bellows may be used to maintain pressure

3.0 Marking of liferafts

3.1   Each liferaft shall be clearly marked with the yacht's name or sail number of identification code on:-

a)   the canopy

b)   the bottom

c)   the valise or container

d)   the certificate

3.2   Numbers and letters on the liferaft should be as large as possible and in a strongly contrasting colour. Marine grade retro-reflective material shall be appropriately fitted to every raft.

ISAF Offshore Special Regulations Appendix A, Part II
Including US SAILING Prescriptions

APPENDIX A part II

Minimum Specifications for Yachtsmen's Liferafts
Appendix A does not cover liferafts intended for category 0 races

1.0   Introduction

In his report of 12/00 and in the absence of a comprehensive up-to-date standard for yachtsmen's liferafts the Sydney Coroner recommended after the Hobart Race 1998 that yachtsmen's liferafts should comply with the construction requirements of Regulation 15 of SOLAS 1960. SOLAS rafts are generally heavier, more expensive and more bulky than yachtsmen's liferafts and are designed for commercial vessels.

In 1999 the ORC Special Regulations Committee (now the Special Regulations sub Committee of ISAF the International Sailing Federation) established a working party to study liferaft specifications taking into account experiences from the Fastnet 79, the Hobart 98 and other sources. The present Appendix A Part II Minimum Specification has drawn on lessons learned.

Although work has been in progress by ISO (the International Standardization Organization) for some 14 years the expected publication of ISO 9650 covering yachtsmen's liferafts, has not taken place. When ISO 9650 is available for public use it will be studied by the Special Regulations sub-Committee with a view to it being accepted in lieu of, or superceding, the Appendix A Part II specification.

In events under ISAF Offshore Special Regulations in categories 0, 1 and 2 liferafts are required. A liferaft for Category 0 shall be a SOLAS model with variations permitted by Special Regulations. A liferaft in categories 1 and 2 shall be either:

(i)   a SOLAS model with variations permitted by Special Regulations, or

(ii)   an "ORC" model in compliance with Special Regulations Appendix A Part I provided the raft was manufactured before 1/03 ***(At least 1/06 in the U.S.)***, or

(iii)   an "ISAF" model in compliance with Special Regulations Appendix A Part II.

ISAF Offshore Special Regulations Appendix A, Part II
Including US SAILING Prescriptions

SPECIFICATIONS FOR YACHTSMEN'S
INFLATABLE LIFERAFTS – Special Regulations Appendix A Part II

PART ONE PURPOSE, CONSTRUCTION and GENERAL

1.1	purpose	The purpose of this specification is to define a yachtsmen's inflatable liferaft which in its design, construction and equipment reflects current best practice and the benefit of hard-won experience in the pursuit of saving life at sea.
1.1.1	strength of build	Every liferaft shall be so constructed as to be capable of withstanding exposure for 20 days afloat in all sea conditions in air temperatures between –15 to +65o C following which the liferaft shall successfully pass the triple-pressure test in 2.03.03 below.
1.2	printed legends and instructions	All printed legends and instructions on the liferaft and its equipment shall be in plain english in letters as large a size as practicable (and may be repeated in another language). Lettering shall be large enough to be easily read by a person with common vision defects and without the aid of spectacles. Printing shall be in a sharply contrasting colour on a plain background.
1.3	persons – definition	Where relevant, for the purposes of this Specification, "persons" will have an average naked weight of 75kg (a single person will have a naked weight of 75kg) and shall wear foul-weather clothing or immersion suits plus sailing boots and also each shall wear an inflated or fully buoyant 150 N lifejacket.
1.4	drop height	The liferaft shall be so constructed that when it is dropped into the water from a height of 6m, the liferaft and its equipment will operate satisfactorily.
1.5	canopy	The liferaft shall have a canopy to protect the occupants from exposure which is automatically set in place when the liferaft is launched and waterborne. The canopy shall remain erected even in the case of deflation of one of the buoyancy chambers.
1.6	canopy insulation	Canopy insulation is optional
1.7	interior colour not to cause discomfort	A blue or other colour for this purpose on the inside of the canopy is optional.

1.8	entrance detail	Each entrance shall be clearly indicated and be provided with efficient adjustable closing arrangements which can be easily and quickly opened from inside and outside, and closed from inside the liferaft so as to permit controlled ventilation but exclude seawater, wind and cold. Liferafts for more than eight persons* shall have at least two independent entrances. Fastening methods for closures may employ easy-to-handle velcro or large zips or, provided they do not depend upon tying or knotting, strings or tapes. Fastening for strings or tapes may be provided by cleats etc. Any closure shall be easy to use with cold, wet, numbed hands. *see 1.3
1.9	ventilation	The canopy shall be capable of admitting sufficient air for the occupants at all times, even with the entrances closed.
1.10	viewing port(s)	The canopy shall be provided with at least one viewing port such that a viewing horizon of 360 degrees is available. Clear plastic windows may be incorporated into the canopy to assist but not to replace this function.
1.11	rainwater collection	The canopy shall be provided with a dedicated means for collecting rainwater. The rainwater collection device shall have an effective means to prevent unwanted ingress of water in heavy weather.
1.12	SART mounting	The canopy shall be provided with means to mount a survival craft radar transponder (SART) at a height of at least 1m above the sea. The mounting shall be clearly marked "SART – SEARCH AND RESCUE RADAR TRANSPONDER"
1.13	canopy height	The canopy shall have sufficient headroom for sitting occupants under all parts.
1.14	carrying capacity	The liferaft shall be constructed to carry up to a specified maximum number of persons* between 4 and 12 inclusive, provided that the specified number does not exceed:- 1.14.1 the greatest whole number obtained by dividing by 0.096 the volume, measured in cubic metres, of the main buoyancy tubes (which for this purpose shall include neither the arches nor the thwarts if fitted) when inflated; or 1.14.2 the greatest whole number obtained by dividing by 0.372 the inner horizontal cross-sectional area of the liferaft measured in square metres (which for this purpose may include the thwart or thwarts if fitted) measured to the innermost edge of the buoyancy tubes; or 1.14.3 the number of persons* that can be seated with reasonable comfort and headroom without interfering with any of the liferaft's equipment.

		1.14.4 the liferaft, inflated to its design operating pressure in calm water, with its largest buoyancy chamber and its inflatable floor (if any) deflated, shall retain positive freeboard when loaded with its full complement of persons* or their equivalent weight evenly distributed. *see 1.3
1.15	Materials	Materials shall comply with the requirements of ISO/DIS 9650-3 as at 2002-02-22 or later
1.16	spare number	
1.17	lifelines interior and exterior	The liferaft shall be equipped with internal and external life-lines made from cordage or webbing which shall be of a bright colour contrasting with the colour of the liferaft, which shall be rot-proof, and resistant to weathering and to oils and petroleum products. They shall be attached to the liferaft in such a manner that, if detached or damaged, the liferaft structure is not damaged. The lifelines shall be able to be grabbed without injuring the hand or slipping. Rope type lifelines shall have a diameter of at least 9.5mm; webbing type lifelines shall be at least 25mm wide. Lifelines and supports shall be capable of withstanding shock-loads and chafe caused by yachtsmens' safety harness being clipped on to the lifeline. The breaking load of a lifeline and of the fastening points shall be at least 2kN.
1.17.1	painter line	1.17.1.1 A painter line shall be provided of >9m in length. The painter line and its attachment shall comprise a system, which is capable of absorbing shock loads without breakage and without damage to the liferaft. 1.17.1.2 The minimum diameter of painter line shall be 9.5mm. The breaking load of the painter line and its attachment to the liferaft shall be not less than 7.5kN or in a raft with capacity of more than 8 persons* the breaking load of the painter line and its attachment to the liferaft shall be not less than 10 kN. 1.17.1.3 The painter line shall withstand weathering and shall be made from nylon or polyester cordage. A coloured indication shall be provided on the painter line at one metre from the firing point.

		1.17.1.4 spare number 1.17.1.5 The painter shall be attached to the liferaft adjacent to an entrance where also a safety knife is provided in a pocket clearly marked "SAFETY KNIFE". *see 1.3
1.18	lamp on canopy	A manually controlled lamp in compliance with IMO MSC 48(66) shall be fitted to the top of the liferaft canopy. Batteries shall be of a type that does not deteriorate due to dampness or humidity in the stowed liferaft.
1.19	lamp inside canopy	Lamp inside canopy is optional
1.20	Construction of buoyancy chambers	The main buoyancy chamber shall be divided into not less than two separate compartments, each inflated through a non-return inflation valve on each compartment.
1.21	floor	1.21.1 The floor of the liferaft shall be waterproof. It is recommended that for operation in cold waters, a means should be provided to insulate the floor. A Race Organiser should specify in the Notice of Race whether insulation may be omitted. 1.21.2 When a floor is insulated with metal foil a notice shall be marked on the floor and also at least once on the inside of the buoyancy tubes where it (they) may best be seen stating: "KEEP ELECTRONIC BEACONS CLEAR OF FLOOR"
	inflation system	1.22.1.1 The initial inflation system shall be actuated by a sharp pull on the painter line, thereby allowing the release of a pressurised gas. All subsequent force exerted on the painter line shall act directly on the towing point or any other point offering strength characteristics equivalent to the values required for the painter line (see 1.17.1). 1.22.1.2 The inflation system mechanism shall attain the fully open position by exerting a pulling force on the painter line not exceeding 150 N and with a travel not exceeding 200 mm. 1.22.1.3 The operating device shall be made of corrosion resistant material capable of withstanding, wtihout damage, a load of 450 N. The operating cable assembly shall not cause any wear of the fabric of the buoyancy chambers by abrasion, and shall conform with the requirements of ISO 15738 inflation systems.
1.22.2	inflation time	The design working pressure shall be achieved within a period of 3 minutes at 20ºC in accordance with the test in 2.11.

1.23.1	resistance to excess pressure (relief valves)	Each inflatable compartment shall be capable of withstanding a pressure equal to at least three times the working pressure and shall be prevented from reaching a pressure exceeding twice the working pressure either by means of relief valves or by a regulated gas supply.) Each valve shall bear marking corresponding to the re-seating pressure (this marking may be a colour code specific to the valve manufacturer).
1.23.2	access to relief valves	Each relief valve shall be accessible to a person* in the liferaft in order to permit the valve to be temporarily sealed off. *see 1.3
1.24	topping up	topping up
1.25	non-return valve	Non-return valves shall be provided at each gas inlet into an inflatable chamber.
1.26	spare number	
1.27	access into raft	At least one entrance shall be fitted with a semi-rigid boarding ramp, capable of supporting a person* weighing 75kg, to enable a person* of not more than average physical ability, unaided to board the liferaft from the sea. The boarding ramp shall be so arranged as to avoid significant deflation of a buoyancy compartment if the ramp is damaged and in any case to limit such deflation so that the pressure in a buoyancy compartment is not caused to fall by more than 50% below its design working pressure. Any high pressure hose or other fitting not intended to be part of the boarding system shall not interfere with the boarding process. *see 1.3
1.28	boarding ladder	Entrances not provided with a boarding ramp shall have a boarding ladder, the lowest step of which shall be weighted and situated not less than 0.4m below the liferaft's light waterline.
1.29	boarding aids	There shall be means inside every entrance to the liferaft to assist persons* to pull themselves into the liferaft: these shall include either a grab line with toggles or other hand-holds, anchored to the far side of the liferaft interior, or to the centre of the floor. Cordage and webbing shall comply with 1.17 above.*see 1.3
1.30	stability of raft	Every inflatable liferaft shall be so constructed that, when fully inflated and floating with the canopy uppermost and with any load from zero up to its full complement of passengers it is stable in a seaway.

1.31	Disymetrical loading	The liferaft, inflated normally under calm sea conditions, shall neither turn over nor be flooded when all the passengers, each wearing a 150 N lifejacket, are grouped together first at any point of the liferaft, then at its opposite point.
1.32	means to right an upturned liferaft	.1 The stability of the liferaft when in the inverted position shall be such that it can be righted in a seaway and in calm water by one person*. .2 Appropriate webbing and/or cordage in compliance with 1.17 above shall be provided on the underside of the liferaft to facilitate the action of one person* in righting an upturned liferaft. .3 The position for a person* in the water to commence righting the liferaft, shall be clearly marked on the buoyancy tube. *see 1.3
1.33	spare number	Each relief valve shall be accessible to a person* in the liferaft in order to permit the valve to be temporarily sealed off. *see 1.3
1.34	ballast pocket(s)	The liferaft shall be fitted with water ballast pocket(s) complying with the following requirements:- 1.34.1 the pocket(s) shall fill(s) to at least 60% of its/their capacity within 25s of deployment. 1.34.2 the pocket(s) shall have an aggregate capacity of at least 220 litres for liferafts certified to carry 4-10 persons* and an aggregate capacity of at least 240 litres for liferafts certified to carry 10-12 persons*. 1.34.3 If more than one pocket they shall be positioned symmetrically round the circumference of the liferaft. If only one pocket its periphery shall be positioned symmetrically round the circumference of the liferaft. 1.34.4 Where appropriate, means shall be provided to enable air to readily escape from underneath the liferaft. *see 1.3

1.35	exterior colour	All exterior surfaces of the liferaft including canopy, ballast pockets, bottom and ramps shall be of a highly visible colour except that the exterior surfaces of buoyancy tubes need not be of a highly visible colour.
1.36	type of gas	The gas or mixture of gases used for inflating the liferafts shall be non-toxic and non-flammable; its moisture content shall not exceed 0,015 % by mass.
1.37	spare	
1.38	spare	
1.39	spare	
1.40	spare	
1.41	gas cylinder	The cylinder, if made of steel, shall conform to ISO 9809-3 unless otherwise authorised by a National Authority. The gas cylinder shall be corrosion-proof. The cylinder shall be marked with its hydraulic test pressure.
1.42	bursting disc	Where a liquefied gas is used, the cylinder shall be fitted with a corrosion-proof bursting disc in accordance with ISO 6718 or with an equivalent safety device to prevent bursting of the cylinder. The bursting disc or the safety device shall operate prior to the internal cylinder pressure reaching the hydraulic test pressure of the cylinder.
1.43	sealing plate	A sealing plate or valve shall be used in order to retain the gas in the cylinder until the liferaft inflation system is actuated. This sealing plate or valve shall withstand the hydraulic test pressure of the cylinder.

1.44	high pressure hose	1.44.1 there shall be no leaks or any sign of deterioration after having been subjected, during at least one minute, to a hydraulic test according to ISO 1402, under a pressure of 12,5 MPa for liquefied gases and or 20 Mpa for non-liquefied gases; 1.44.2 it shall operate within a temperature range between -45 and +65oC inclusive for liquefied gases, between -20 and +65oC inclusive for non-liquefied gases. 1.44.3 at the lowest temperature of each of the ranges defined in 1.44.2 above, the hose shall be bent through 180o over a 5 cm radius mandrel and shall meet the requirements of 1.44.1. 1.44.4 the hose assembly shall not be in contact with any sharp edges and shall not show any sign of corrosion when tested in accordance with the appropriate test defined by the ISO (a new hose may be used for each operating test). 1.44.5 the bursting pressure of the hose assembly shall be not less than 168% of the hydraulic test pressure of the hose assembly. 1.44.6 a high pressure hose shall be installed in such a manner as to avoid impeding the boarding operation (see 1.27 above).
1.45	raft markings certificate	The liferaft and its container or valise, and also an accompanying certificate which shall be kept on board the yacht shall show the following information. Markings on the liferaft shall be in a readily visible location, in a clear and indelible manner and shall have no harmful effect on adjacent materials. All written instructions shall be in the English language and may be repeated in any other language. It is permitted to mark this information on a seawater-resistant label securely attached to the liferaft in a prominent position: .1 number of persons* .2 manufacturer's name .3 raft type name if any .4 "conforms to ISAF OSR Appendix A Part II " plus a description of any optional extras fitted (eg insulated floor, enhanced contents pack)

		.5 date of last service and identity of service station .6 recommended service interval .7 max launching height .8 painter line length .9 launching instructions .10 serial number (see 6.2 identification) .12 date of manufacture .13 any optional features installed :- .13.1 insulated floor Y/N? .13.2 insulated canopy Y/N? .13.3.special interior colour Y/N? .13.4 interior lamp Y/N? .14 list of contents of equipment pack *see 1.3
1.46	spare	
1.47	spare	
1.48	equipment pockets	At least two equipment pockets shall be provided made from transparent flexible plastic material with drain holes and provided with velcro flaps, appropriately fixed to a canopy arch tube. Purpose is to stow loose equipment where it can be seen and kept readily available but safe against loss and as far as possible away from constant wetting.
1.49	retro-reflective material	A minimum surface area of 1500 cm2 of reflective material shall be attached to each liferaft. Around 2/3 of this material surface shall be fixed to the upper half of the canopy and approximately 1/3 to the outer part of the liferaft bottom. The reflective material must comply with IMO A.658 (16).

2.0	**PART TWO TESTING**	The following tests shall be satisfactorily completed on a representative sample of each raft. Weights used in the tests may be eg bags filled with water or sand.
2.1	launching test	Position the complete liferaft, packed in its valise or container, at a height of 6m above the water. Attach the painter line to a fixed point so that it pays out when the liferaft drops. Let the liferaft drop into the water and leave it to float for 30 minutes, then inflate it by pulling on the painter line. Measure the time taken: 2.1.1 by the buoyancy chambers to inflate to their final shape and for the canopy to fully deploy 2.1.2 to reach the design working pressure. Remove the liferaft from the water. Thoroughly inspect the liferaft and its equipment. There shall be no detectable damage or deterioration.
2.2	capacity test	Verify by an actual test with the raft afloat that the stated number of persons* can be accommodated each in a seated position. *see 1.3
2.2.1	minimum freeboard test	Inflate the liferaft to normal working pressure and under calm sea conditions load the liferaft uniformly with 75 kg weights equal to the number of persons* which is the rated capacity. The freeboard measured at various peripheral points shall be at least 250 mm on a 4-person* capacity liferaft and 300 mm for all larger liferafts. *see 1.3
2.3.1	pressure maintenanc e test for buoyancy chambers and canopy support	Inflate to the design working pressure, then leave to stand for 30 minutes. Readjust, if necessary, the design working pressure, note the ambient temperature, wait 1 hour and record the measured final pressure and the ambient temperature. Apply if necessary a correction taking account of the variation in temperature at the rate of 0.4 kPa per degree centigrade. The final pressure, corrected if necessary, shall not be less than 95 % of the initial pressure. The test is only valid if the temperature variation within the chamber is less than or equal to 3oC.
2.3.2	pressure maintenan-ce test for inflatable floor (if fitted)	Inflate to the design working pressure, wait 30 minutes and record the final pressure, which shall be not less than 95% of the design working pressure.

2.3.3	excess pressure test	Inflate the buoyancy chambers and the canopy to 3 times the design working pressure at a temperature of 20+/- 2oC and wait 10 minutes. The relief valves shall be rendered inoperable during this test. Record the final pressure, which shall be not less than 95% of the design working pressure. Thoroughly inspect the liferaft and its equipment. There shall be no detectable damage or deterioration.
2.4	flooding resistance test	.1 The liferaft, inflated to its design working pressure and under calm water conditions shall carry its full load of persons* If an inflatable floor is fitted this shall be deflated. .2 The liferaft shall then be filled with water to the top of the upper buoyancy chamber and maintained in this condition for 10 minutes. .3 The liferaft shall not suffer any deformation during this test. Thoroughly inspect the liferaft and its equipment. There shall be no detectable damage or deterioration. *see 1.3
2.5	jumping test	The liferaft, in calm water conditions and inflated to its design working pressure, shall be able to withstand without any detectable damage or deterioration the falling onto the canopy and into a liferaft entrance (in both closed and open conditions) of a weight of 75 kg from a height of 3 metres above the water level. The total number of "drops" shall be equal to the rated carrying capacity of the liferaft.
2.6	3 knot tow streaming sea anchor	.1 Inflate the liferaft to the design working pressure in calm water and deploy the sea anchor. Load the liferaft with its full complement of persons* or with an equivalent number of 75 kg weights. .2 Secure a tow line to the yacht end of the painter line so that the total length of the tow line is 30m (do not include the painter line's weak link device in the section which will bear the towing load). .3 For an overall period of at least 30 minutes, tow the liferaft at a speed of 3 knots, whilst:-. .3.1 stopping and resuming towing, jerking forward several times. .4 During the test:- .4.1 the sea anchor shall remain deployed in a stable position beneath the water surface .4.2 the sea anchor shall not become tangled in its shroud lines

		.4.3 the minimum traction exerted on the sea anchor during towing shall be 450 N .5 the liferaft shall not capsize or become flooded. .6 After the towing test:-.6.1 a tensile test shall be performed on the sea anchor line and its attachment. The breaking load of the sea anchor line and its attachment shall be >5 kN .6.2 a tensile test shall be performed on the painter line and its attachment. The breaking load of the painter line and its attachment shall be >5 kN .6.2 thoroughly inspect the liferaft and its equipment. There shall be no detectable damage or deterioration. *see 1.3
2.7	paddling test	The liferaft, in calm sea conditions and normally inflated, loaded with it full load of passengers each wearing a foul-weather suit and a 150 N lifejacket and seaboots, shall be able to move forward under the action of the passengers with the supplied paddles, at a speed of at least 0.5 knots over a distance of at least 20 metres.
2.8	canopy watertightness test	The liferaft, in calm water conditions and inflated to its design working pressure, shall be able to withstand without any detectable damage or deterioration the falling onto the canopy and into a liferaft entrance (in both closed and open conditions) of a weight of 75 kg from a height of 3 metres above the water level. The total number of "drops" shall be equal to the rated carrying capacity of the liferaft.
2.9	spare	
2.10	stability during boarding test	.1 The liferaft shall be inflated to its design working pressure and deployed in calm water .2 Three persons* shall take part in the test. .3 Two persons* on board the liferaft shall be capable of taking on board a third person* floating on his or her back, without the liferaft being capsized or flooded. *see 1.3
2.11	inflation test at ambient temperature	.1 Let the liferaft packed in its valise or container stand for 24 hours at an ambient temperature of 20 +/- 2oC. .2 Inflate the liferaft by pulling on the painter line. .3 The buoyancy chambers shall be inflated to their final shape and the canopy deployed within 60 seconds of actuating the inflation device. .4 The design working pressure shall be achieved within 3 minutes of actuating the inflation device.

2.12	inflation test at high temperature	.1 Let the liferaft packed in its valise or container stand in a heating chamber for at least 7 hours.
		.2 The chamber temperature shall have reached 65oC in less than 2 hours and shall be maintained at this value during the remainder of the 7 hours.
		.3 Note: it is preferable to heat up the liferaft in a chamber large enough to be able to inflate it therein, but it is also permitted to remove it from the chamber after 7 hours heating up, provided that it is inflated as early as possible after withdrawal.
		.4 Inflate the liferaft by pulling on the painter line. Check that the pressure relief valves are operating suitably. Record the maximum pressure in the buoyancy chambers.
		.5 The maximum pressure in any buoyancy chamber during the test shall not exceed twice the design working pressure.
		.6 Thoroughly inspect the liferaft and its equipment. There shall be no detectable damage or deterioration.
2.13	inflation test at low temperature	.1 Let the liferaft packed in its valise or container stand in a cold chamber for at least 24 hours at a temperature of −15oC. The tests in .2 .3 and .4 below shall be carried out on the liferaft within the cold chamber.
		.2 Inflate the liferaft by pulling on the painter line.
		.3 The buoyancy chambers shall be inflated to their design working pressure and the canopy deployed within 5 minutes of actuating the inflation device.
		.4 Thoroughly inspect the liferaft and its equipment. There shall be no detectable damage or deterioration.
2.14.1	ballast pocket strength test (when more than one pocket is installed)	.1 Inflate the liferaft to the design working pressure, supporting it in the air in such a manner that 2 water pockets, on opposite sides and as near as possible to the periphery of the liferaft, are suspended freely with a 300 mm space between the support and the pocket attachment.
		.2 Load each water pocket with a weight equivalent to three times the mass of water that they can contain and maintain this test condition for at least one hour.
		.3 Thoroughly inspect the water pockets and attachments. There shall be no detectable damage or deterioration.
2.14.2	ballast pocket strength test (single-pocket liferaft)	A test similar in effect to that in 2.14.1 shall be specified by the manufacturer and carried out satisfactorily.

2.12	inflation test at high temperature	.1 Let the liferaft packed in its valise or container stand in a heating chamber for at least 7 hours. .2 The chamber temperature shall have reached 65oC in less than 2 hours and shall be maintained at this value during the remainder of the 7 hours. .3 Note: it is preferable to heat up the liferaft in a chamber large enough to be able to inflate it therein, but it is also permitted to remove it from the chamber after 7 hours heating up, provided that it is inflated as early as possible after withdrawal. .4 Inflate the liferaft by pulling on the painter line. Check that the pressure relief valves are operating suitably. Record the maximum pressure in the buoyancy chambers. .5 The maximum pressure in any buoyancy chamber during the test shall not exceed twice the design working pressure. .6 Thoroughly inspect the liferaft and its equipment. There shall be no detectable damage or deterioration.
2.13	inflation test at low temperature	.1 Let the liferaft packed in its valise or container stand in a cold chamber for at least 24 hours at a temperature of –15oC. The tests in .2 .3 and .4 below shall be carried out on the liferaft within the cold chamber. .2 Inflate the liferaft by pulling on the painter line. .3 The buoyancy chambers shall be inflated to their design working pressure and the canopy deployed within 5 minutes of actuating the inflation device. .4 Thoroughly inspect the liferaft and its equipment. There shall be no detectable damage or deterioration.
2.14.1	ballast pocket strength test (when more than one pocket is installed)	.1 Inflate the liferaft to the design working pressure, supporting it in the air in such a manner that 2 water pockets, on opposite sides and as near as possible to the periphery of the liferaft, are suspended freely with a 300 mm space between the support and the pocket attachment. .2 Load each water pocket with a weight equivalent to three times the mass of water that they can contain and maintain this test condition for at least one hour. .3 Thoroughly inspect the water pockets and attachments. There shall be no detectable damage or deterioration.
2.14.2	ballast pocket strength test (single-pocket liferaft)	A test similar in effect to that in 2.14.1 shall be specified by the manufacturer and carried out satisfactorily.

2.14.3	ballast pocket deployment test	.1 Inflate the liferaft to its design working pressure, in calm water of temperature not exceeding 4°C. .2 After 25 seconds lift the liferaft from the water and measure the amount of water collected in the ballast pockets, which shall in the case of each pocket be at least 60% of its capacity. 3. A similar test may be defined by the manufacturer of a single-pocket liferaft and shall be carried out satisfactorily.
2.15	righting test	.1 Inflate the liferaft to its design working pressure, in a swimming pool in water of >3m depth .2 Overturn the liferaft. A righting strop should reach the water. Provide 4 persons* in turn to attempt to right the liferaft. The persons* shall preferably not be good swimmers, shall have different physiques, and shall comprise two male and two female. For each righting attempt the liferaft shall have no persons* inside. .3 Each person* shall swim 50 metres before attempting to right the liferaft and there shall be no rest period between the swimming and the righting attempt. .4 Each person* shall be able to right the liferaft unaided. *see 1.3
3.0	**PART THREE RAFT CONTAINER**	
3.1	container general	The liferaft shall be packed in a valise or hard container which is:- .1 so constructed as to withstand hard wear under conditions encountered at sea .2 of sufficient inherent buoyancy when packed to enable the upthrust of the inherent buoyancy to pull the painter from within the container and to operate the inflation mechanism should the parent yacht sink .3 as far as practicable watertight, except for drain holes in the container bottom .4 clearly marked on the outside with the intended stowage attitude (eg "THIS WAY UP") .5 clearly marked on the side intended to be uppermost "NO STEP"

		.6 so arranged as to ensure, as far as possible, that the waterborne liferaft inflates in an upright position on breaking free from its container .7 provided with carrying handles or other means to enable the unit to be manhandled with reasonable ease .8 capable of providing the liferaft and its equipment with adequate protection in conditions of prolonged stowage on board.
3.2	printed instructions for the yacht	Instructions, printed on durable waterproof medium in large clear type shall be provided stating:- .1 how to stow the liferaft the correct side up, in an appropriate stowage (see SR 4.20 and secure the painter (note the weak link) .2 the location of the grab bag(s) .3 what else is recommended to take into the liferaft .4 a reminder to send a distress message by the yacht's main radio or satcom before leaving .5 importance not to launch the liferaft until absolutely necessary in order to minimise risk of damage .6 how to launch the liferaft .7 how to right the liferaft .8 diagram of the raft with locations of knife, sea anchor, lifebuoy (throwing line) and inflation points .9 importance of fittest individual being first person* to board the raft, to help others get in .10 the date of the next required service .11 first measures –see 4.15.6 below. *see 1.3
4.0	**PART FOUR EQUIPMENT PACKED INSIDE RAFT**	The following minimum equipment shall be provided appropriately packed inside the liferaft. (This list closely but not precisely follows that of SOLAS B).
4.1	general	4.1.1 Every package, closure and item of equipment shall be:- 4.1.1.1 capable of being opened and re-sealed easily and used with cold, wet, numbed hands and without an implement of any kind

		4.1.1.2 impervious to water and rust. 4.1.2 Every package shall have readily re-sealable closures of velcro, large zips, captive elastic shockcord loops. shockcords or cords with jamb cleats, or other suitable methods. 4.1.3 .Portable items shall be capable of being fitted into installed pockets provided in the interior of the liferaft. 4.1.4 Portable items shall have lanyard or tape "tails" with velcro self-seal strips at the ends to facilitate making captive without tying knots 4.1.5 Portable items shall (except where essential) be without sharp corners, sharp edges and unnecessary protrusions which could injure survivors or cause damage to the liferaft fabric. 4.1.6 The equipment pack shall be inherently buoyant, brightly coloured and captive by a line to the inside of the raft. Instructions shall be marked on each item as appropriate (see 1.2).
4.2	rescue throwing line min 30m	A rescue throwing line of min breaking strain 1.0kN and length >30m shall be stowed in a re-useable "throwing sock".
4.3	safety knife in pocket	One non-folding safety knife with buoyant handle and lanyard attached in a pocket on the exterior of the canopy adjacent to the fixing point of the painter line. Both knife and pocket shall be clearly marked "SAFETY KNIFE"
4.4	bailer	One portable buoyant bailer, clearly marked "BAILER". If a sleeve bailer (optional) is permanently fitted in the floor of the liferaft the portable bailer shall be provided as a spare.
4.5	sponges	One sponge for each person
4.6	sea anchor	At least one sea anchor to ISO 17339 equipped with at least one swivel connected to the raft so that it will stream on deployment. Diameter of line to be not less than 9.5mm to make it easy to handle. The line shall be >30m in length. The sea anchor, line and fixing arrangement to the liferaft, must be capable of withstanding heavy shock loads as described in 1.17.1.2 painter criteria. When only one sea anchor is carried in the liferaft a second sea anchor shall be carried in the yacht's grab bag.
4.7	2 buoyant paddles	Two buoyant paddles with handles (not mitts) tied into raft adjacent to an entrance. The location of the paddles shall be indicated in large clear lettering on the outside and the inside of the canopy.

4.8	first aid kit	A basic first-aid kit shall include at least 2 tubes of sunscreen and 1 tube of sunburn treatment cream. If water is not included in the liferaft kit, at least 0.5 litre to aid taking seasickness or analgesic tablets etc shall be provided in a soft plastic drinking pack with a built-in valve. Small bottle caps etc shall if possible be captive to aid the action of re-sealing. All dressings shall if possible be capable of being effectively used in wet conditions. The first-aid kit shall be clearly marked and it is recommended, should fit into a prepared and clearly marked stowage pocket.
4.9	whistle or bull horn	At least one.
4.10	torches	2 waterproof sealed-for-life torches. Each torch shall be sealed in clearly marked packaging, which prevents the operation of the torch until the packaging is removed. Torch packaging shall be clearly marked with the expiry date of the torch. Each torch shall be capable of providing a continuous light of 6 hours.
4.11	spare	
4.12	signal mirror	A signalling mirror shall be provided clearly marked with instructions.
4.13	copy of the lifesaving signal code	In accordance with SOLAS regulation V/16
4.14	seasick pills	min 6 per person
4.14.1	seasick bags	1 seasick bag per person with a simple effective closure system
4.15	survival instruction-s	Printed instructions on durable waterproof medium written in plain english (see 1.2 above) shall include the following:- .1 the list of equipment packed in the raft .2 use of the liferaft .3 how to survive on board .4 how to right the liferaft after a capsize .5 diagram of liferaft with locations of knife, painter fixing, sea anchor, throwing line, equipment and PLB pockets and all inflation points. .6 first measures to be taken ie .6.1 disengage the painter line and move clear of the parent vessel .6.2 deploy the sea ancho to resist capsize

		.6.3 close the liferaft entrance maintain the liferaft in good condition by bailing, inflate or deploy the insulated bottom (if fitted and if requiring manual deployment), checking for and repairing leaks, etc. .6.4 deploy PLB appropriately and maintain watch etc.
4.16	red flares	3 red hand flares in accordance with SOLAS regulation 36.
4.17	2 thermal protective aids (survival bags)	In accordance with SOLAS LSA 2.5 (waterproof, and designed to reduce convective and evaporative heat loss from the wearer's body).
4.18	repair outfit	To enable persons* with numbed, wet, cold hands to repair leaks in the inflatable compartments including eg buoyancy tubes, inflatable floor (if fitted), inflatable canopy support (if fitted), inflatable boarding ramp (if fitted). Repair systems must work when wet and be capable of being applied during violent motion. The repair outfit shall include at least 6 leak-stop pugs. *see 1.3
4.19	air pump	must be simple, robust, and complete with all necessary connections (loose parts must be captive to the main apparatus) ready for instant use to enable persons* with numbed, wet, cold hands to pump air into the inflatable compartments including eg buoyancy tubes, inflatable floor (if fitted), inflatable canopy support (if fitted), inflatable boarding ramp (if fitted). The air pump must be designed and built specifically for easy operation by hand.
4.20	spare number	
4.21	"wet" notebook and pencil	A notebook shall be supplied with toughened paper designed to be capable of use in wet conditions. A pencil shall be provided captive to the "wet" notebook.
4.22	paddles, torch and instructions to be immediately available	Of the equipment items listed above, the paddles, torch and instructions shall be immediately and obviously available to a survivor on boarding the liferaft.

US Edition 2004 - 2005
ISAF Offshore Special Regulations Appendix A, Part II
Including US SAILING Prescriptions

5.0	**PART FIVE GRAB BAG**	The liferaft is designed to be complemented by the grab bag described in Special Regulations
6.0	**PART SIX**	**DOCUMENTATION, MAKERS' MARKS, SERVICING**
6.1	service record sheet on waterproof medium	One copy shall be stowed inside liferaft container. A second copy shall be provided to be kept inside the yacht.
6.2	Liferaft identification	A unique serial number (which may comprise a set of numbers and letters) shall be marked in strongly contrasting colour and as large as possible on the outside of the canopy and on the outside of the bottom; this serial number shall be marked also on the certificate and on the outside of the valise or container.

6.3	servicing general	With the aim of guaranteeing correct operation and maintenance of the quality of the equipment during its entire lifetime, liferafts shall be regularly serviced by manufacturer-approved service stations. Manufacturers are responsible for: .1 ensuring that their liferafts are designed and constructed to be serviced in accordance with their recommendations .2 approving a sufficient number of service stations .3 ensuring that each of their approved service stations has staff suitably trained, qualified and certificated and familiar with all changes and new techniques introduced by the manufacturer .4 placing at the disposal of the service stations- .4.1 servicing manual(s) (see 6.4.3 below) .4.2 modifications to the servicing manual(s) and also appropriate bulletins and instructions .4.3 appropriate materials and spare parts
6.4	servicing	Liferafts shall be serviced every 12 months after a possible period without servicing defined below. .1 When designed and built to have an extended period between initial services the liferaft may provided the manufacturer clearly specifies the intervals, have its first service no longer than 3 years after commissioning and its second service no longer than 2 years after the first. Subsequent services, and services for all other liferafts, shall be at intervals of not more than 12 months. .2 At each service inspection shall be made of- .2.1 the structure .2.2 the inflation system .2.3 the emergency equipment (eg torches) .2.4 the liferaft equipment (eg ladders, lines, sea anchor(s))

		.3 A detailed list of the points to be serviced, the procedures to be followed, the items to be replaced etc. shall be clearly set out in the servicing manual supplied to the service station and which may be consulted by the public. All items having an expiry date shall be replaced when this date would occur prior to the next scheduled service. All inspections carried out shall be recorded and the records maintained by the service station.
7.0	**PART SEVEN**	**LIFERAFT STOWAGE**
7.1		Liferaft stowage in offshore racing is subject to Special Regulation 4.20
8.0	**PART EIGHT**	**QUALITY ASSURANCE**
8.1	guality assurance	*A liferaft manufactured in or after 1/04 should be produced in compliance with ISO 9001:2000.* A liferaft manufactured in or after 1/05 shall be produced in compliance with ISO 9001:2000.

APPENDIX B
A Guide to ISO and other standards

Application and Development Policy
Whenever possible a relevant ISO Standard, CEN Norm, SOLAS regulation or other internationally-recognized standard is called up by Special Regulations. Changes and developments in international standards are reviewed by the Special Regulations sub Committee and may replace part of Special Regulations. Significant changes will when possible affect new yachts and/or new equipment only.

ISO
ISO, the International Organization for Standardization is a world-wide federation of national standards bodies (ISO member bodies). The work of preparing International Standards is normally carried out through ISO Technical Committees. Each member body interested in a subject for which a Technical Committee has been established has the right to be represented on that committee. International organizations governmental and non-governmental, including eg ISAF, take part in the work. Copies of International Standards may be obtained from a national standards body.
The following International Standards (or Draft Standards) are mentioned in Special Regulations:-

ISO standard	subject	SR
12217-2	assessment of stability and buoyancy	3.04.4, 3.05
11812	watertight & quick draining cockpits	3.09
15085	guardlines (lifelines) trampolines, nets, stanchions, hooking points	3.14, 3.15
8729	marine radar reflectors	4.10
9650	liferafts	Appendix A Part II
12401	deck safety harness (also published as EN 1095)	5.02
12215	hull construction standards	3.03
17339	sea anchors	4.21.2 (i)

ISAF Offshore Special Regulations Appendix B
Including US SAILING Prescriptions

CEN

CEN standards (Norms) are developed in Europe by CEN (European Committee for Standardization - Committée Européen de Normalisation) which publishes ENs (European Norms) and which works closely with ISO. In Special Regulations the following are mentioned:-

EN standard	Subject	SR
394,399	lifejacket accessories	5.01
396	lifejackets	5.01
1095	deck safety harness (also published as ISO 12401)	5.02
1913-1-3	immersion suits	5.07

ABS

ABS Guide for Building and Classing Offshore Yachts. This Guide to scantlings (construction standards) was originally published by ABS (American Bureau of Shipping) in co-operation with the Offshore Racing Council. A plan approval service formerly offered by ABS has been discontinued. However, copies of the Guide are available from the ISAF office. Designers and builders may provide written statements to confirm that they have designed and built a yacht in accordance with the original Guide or ABS-approved derivatives (see SR 3.03.1(b)). Work on ISO 12215 (which may become a new minimum standard in Special Regulations) is in progress.

RCD

The RCD (Recreational Craft Directive) is published with the authority of the EC under which "nominating bodies" including some maritime classification societies and in the UK and Ireland, the RYA (Royal Yachting Association) and the IYA (Irish Yachting Association), may approve construction standards of yachts which may then be entitled to display a CE mark permitting sale in the EC (see SR 3.03.1(a)). Work on ISO 12215 (which may become a new minimum standard in Special Regulations) is in progress.

SOLAS

The SOLAS (Safety of Life At Sea) Convention is published by IMO (International Maritime Organization) at which ISAF has Consultative Status. SOLAS Chapter III, Regulation 3, 10 refers to the LSA (Life Saving Appliances) Code (published as a separate booklet) to which Special Regulations makes the following references:-

Addresses

LSA Code	Subject	SR
Chapter III, 3.1, 3.2, 3.3	flares (pyrotechnics)	4.23
Chapter II, 2.2.3	lifejacket lights	5.01
Chapter IV, 4	liferafts	4.20
Chapter II, 2.3	immersion suits	5.07.1
Chapter II, 2.5	thermal protective aids	Appendix A Part 2

CEN Central Secretariat,
rue de Stassart 36,
B-1050 Brussels,
Belgium
tel +32 2 550 08 11
fax +32 2 550 08 19
www.cenom.be

ISO Central Secretariat,
1 rue de Varembé,
Case Postale 56,
CH-1211 Genéve 20,
Switzerland
email: central@isocs.iso.ch
tel +41 22 749 01 11
fax + 41 22 733 34 30
www.iso.ch

IMO International Maritime Organization,
4 Albert Embankment,
London EC1 7SR,
Great Britain
email: info@imo.org
tel +44 207 735 7611
fax +44 207 587 3210
www.imo.org

APPENDIX C

STANDARD INSPECTION CARD p1 of 2

Please note that this appendix is not comprehensive but only a guide for use by Race Organisers.
Add items as appropriate. A copy of the card should be given to the yacht in advance.

OWNERS please prepare the boat and sign the card.
INSPECTORS mark each item with a tick or cross in the check box. Write an additional report if necessary.
Show card to the owner and return card with report to the Race Committee as soon as possible.

YACHT _____ Sail No _____

Number of crew this race _____ Liferaft total capacity _____

IMPORTANT inspection is carried out only as a guide to owners. An inspector cannot limit or reduce the complete and unlimited responsibility of the owner or owner's representative.

"I hereby declare that I am the owner or owner's representative and that I have read and understood Special Regulations and in particular 1.02.1, 1.02.2, and 1.02.3 (owner's responsibility)"

Signed _____ Printed name _____

Date _____

Below Deck

	SR	
on one or more berths show the following:- _____		
all safety harness and lines_____ how many? ☐ _____	5.02.1	☐
coloured flags in new harness lines? _____	5.02	☐
all safety harness lines extra_____ how many? ☐	5.02.2	☐
all lifejackets _____ how many? ☐ _____	5.01	☐
foghorn_____	4.09	☐
flashlight + spare batteries and bulbs _____	4.07.1(b)	☐
hi-powered flashlight/spotlight + appropriate spares_____	4.07.1(a)	☐
rigging cutters _____	4.16	☐
first aid kit and manual_____	4.08	☐
2 stout buckets _____	3.23	☐
2 fire extinguishers_____	4.05	☐
is keel-stepped mast heel restrained? _____	3.12	☐
engine permanently installed and securely covered? _____	3.28.1	☐
heavy-weather jib (if not rigged on deck-see below) _____	4.26.4 (b), (f)	☐
stowage chart with location of principal items of safety equipment _____	4.12	☐
heavy movable objects securely fastened in place?_____	2.03.2	☐

also show the following:-

			SR		
valid liferaft certificate(s)_____ how many? ☐ (see heading)			4.20.4	in date? _____	☐
rating certificate(s) (signed by owner)? ☐ expiry date? _____					
radar reflector data sheet (if not 18" octahedral) declaring at least 10m2 RCS _____			4.10		☐
charts (not solely electronic) _____			4.11		☐

73

US Edition 2004 - 2005
ISAF Offshore Special Regulations Appendix C
Including US SAILING Prescriptions

STANDARD INSPECTION CARD p2 of 2

SR _____

ABS approved plans or compliance statement from designer _____	3.03.1 _____	☐
ABS compliance statement from builder _____	3.03.1 _____	☐
406MHz EPIRB - identity number? _____ serviced? ☐ _____	4.19 _____	☐
Statement(s) of training completed by how many crew? _____	6.01 _____	☐

On Deck

block companionway hatch shut _____	3.08.3(b) _____	☐
show retaining device connected to washboard(s) _____	3.08.4(b)(ii) _____	☐
show retaining device connected to bilge pump handle(s) _____	3.23.4 _____	☐
"rig the storm jib (or if none, the heavy weather jib) with sheets ready for use" _____	4.26.4(a),(e) _____	☐
rig the trysail with sheets ready for use _____	4.26.4(a),(e) _____	☐
can trysail be set without removing mainsail from luff groove or mainsail cars from track? _____	4.26.4(a),(e) _____	☐
install equipment for steering without the rudder - has it been tried? _____	4.15.1(b) _____	☐
rig radar reflector at least 4.0m above the water as it would be used _____	4.10 _____	☐
prepare to demonstrate nav lights both main and reserve _____	3.27 _____	☐
fix shut cockpit lockers as if for heavy weather _____	3.02.1 _____	☐
can crew stay clipped on along and across deck? _____	4.04.2(b)(ii) _____	☐
are lifelines taut? _____	3.14.2 _____	☐
show jackstays rigged for use _____	4.04 _____	☐
static safety lines at work stations? how many? _____	4.04.2(b) & 5.02.5(b) _____	☐

Man Overboard

date and place of last MoB drill? _____	6.04.1 _____	☐
how many of this crew has done MoB drill on this boat? _____	6.04.1 _____	☐

Pyrotechnics (flares)

remove each flare from container and have laid out for inspection. _____	4.23 _____	☐
red hand flares -how many? All SOLAS? _____	4.23 _____	☐
red parachute flares -how many? All SOLAS? _____	4.23 _____	☐
white hand flares -how many? _____	4.23 _____	☐
orange smoke flares -how many? All SOLAS? _____	4.23 _____	☐
can crew members describe ""blind"" how these flares operate? _____	4.23 _____	☐

Inspector's Report to Race Committee

I inspected the above yacht on _____ (date) at _____ (place)

Comments: _____

_____

_____

Signed _____ Printed name _____

APPENDIX D
For information only
Quickstop and Lifesling

MAN OVERBOARD – QUICK STOP AND THE LIFE SLING
(OR SEATTLE SLING)
When a crew member goes over the side recovery time is of the essence. In an effort to come up with a recovery system that is simple and lightning quick, the US Yacht Racing Union Safety at
Sea Committee, the US Naval Academy Sailing Squadron, the
Cruising Club of America Technical Committee and the Sailing
Foundation of Seattle, Washington, joined forces to conduct extensive research and sea trials. The result of their collaboration is the "Quick-Stop" method of man-overboard recovery.
The hallmark of this method is the immediate reduction of boat speed by turning to windward and then manoeuvring slowly,
remaining near the victim. In most cases, this is better than reaching off, then gybing or tacking and returning on a reciprocal course.

QUICK-STOP

1. Shout "man overboard" and detail a crew member to spot and point to **the victim's position** in the water. The spotter should not take his eyes off the victim (see Figure 1).

2. Provide immediate flotation. Throw buoyant objects such as cockpit cushions, life rings and so on. These objects may not only come to the aid of the victim, but will "litter the water" where he went overboard and help your spotter to keep him in view. Deployment of the pole and flag (dan buoy) requires too much time. The pole is saved to "put on top" of the victim in case the initial manoeuvre is unsuccessful.

3. Bring boat head-to-wind and beyond (see Figure 1).

4. Allow headsail to back and further slow the boat.

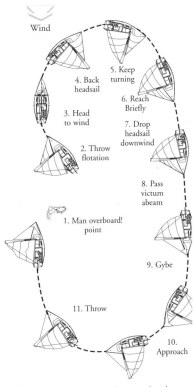

Wind

1. Man overboard! point
2. Throw flotation
3. Head to wind
4. Back headsail
5. Keep turning
6. Reach Briefly
7. Drop headsail downwind
8. Pass victum abeam
9. Gybe
10. Approach
11. Throw

Figure 1. Twelve steps to a quick manoverboard recovery.

5. Keep turning with headsail backed until wind is abaft the beam.

6. Head on beam-to-broad reach course for two or three lengths then go nearly dead downwind.

7. Drop the headsail while keeping the mainsail centered (or nearly so). The jib sheets are not slacked, even during the dousing manoeuvre, to keep them inside the lifelines.

8. Hold the downward course until victim is abaft the beam.

9. Gybe.

10. Approach the victim on a course of **approximately** 45 degrees to 60 degrees off the wind.

11. Establish contact with the victim with heaving line or other device. The Naval Academy uses a "throwing sock" containing 75 feet of light floating line and a bag that can be thrown into the wind because the line is kept inside the bag and trails out as it sails to the victim.

12. Effect recovery over the windward side.

Quickstop Under Spinnaker

The same procedure is used to accommodate a spinnaker.

Follow the preceding instructions. As the boat comes head-to-wind and the pole is eased to the head stay, the spinnaker halyard is lowered and the sail is gathered on the fore deck. The turn is continued through the tack and the approach phase commences.

Quickstop in Yawls & Ketches

Experiment with your mizzensail. During sea trials, it was found best to drop the mizzen as soon as possible during the early phases of Quick-Stop.

Quickstop Using Engine

Use of the engine is not essential, although it's advisable to have it running in neutral, during Quick-Stop in case it is needed in the final approach. Check first for trailing lines!

ISAF Offshore Special Regulations Appendix D
Including US SAILING Prescriptions

SHORTHANDED CREWS

When there are only two people sailing together and a man-overboard accident occurs, the remaining crew member may have difficulty in handling the recovery alone. If the victim has sustained injuries, getting him back aboard may be almost impossible. The Quick-Stop method is simple to effect by a
singlehander, with only one alteration to the procedure: the addition of the "Lifesling", a floating horsecollar device that doubles as a hoisting sling. The Lifesling is attached to the boat by a length of floating line three or four times the boat's length.
When a crew member falls overboard the scenario should proceed as follows:
1. A cushion or other flotation is thrown while the boat is brought IMMEDIATELY head-to-wind, slowed and stopped
(Figure 2 below).

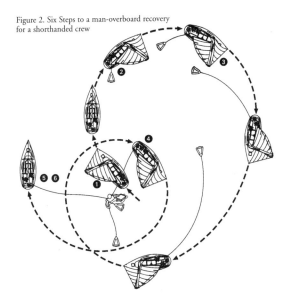

Figure 2. Six Steps to a man-overboard recovery for a shorthanded crew

2. The Lifesling is deployed by opening the bag on the stern pulpit and dropping the sling into the water. It will trail astern and draw out the line.
3. Attach a three-or four-part tackle to the main halyard, haul it up to a predetermined point, about 10 feet above the deck or high enough so that the victim can be hoisted up and over the lifelines. Cleat off the halyard.
4. Attach the lower end of the tackle to the (previouslysized) loop in the tether line that passes through the D-rings of the sling.

ISAF Offshore Special Regulations Appendix D
Including US SAILING Prescriptions

Figure 4.

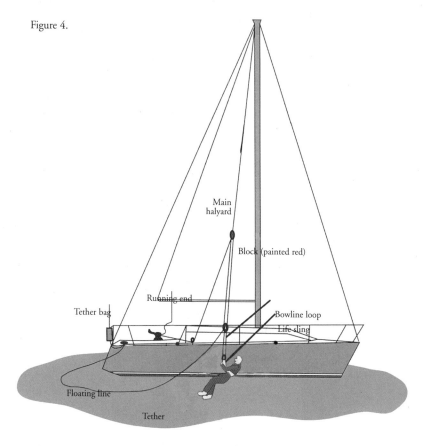

5. Reeve the running end of the tackle through a sheet block or snatch block on deck and put it on a cockpit winch. Hoist the victim aboard by winching it on the running end of the tackle.

PARBUCKLE DEVICE

This is an alternative to the hoisting rig. A patent version is known as the Tri-buckle. Another version is rectangular, like a climbing net. The net, or triangle of strong porous material, is clipped to the toe rail, the triangle top or net extremity clipped to a halyard extension. The casualty is manoevred or dragged alongside into the triangle or net then rolled onto the deck by hoisting the halyard.

Hypothermic aftershock may be minimized by this method which keeps the casualty essentially horizontal.

APPENDIX E

HYPOTHERMIA

WHAT IS IT?

A condition in which exposure to cold air and/or water lowers body core temperature. Death can result from too low a brain and heart temperature.

WHY BE CONCERNED?

Hypothermia, even mild cases, decreases crew efficiency and increases risk of costly accidents. *Proper planning against hypothermia can give a winning competitive edge.*

PREVENTION

● Wear warm clothing and a lifejacket/harness. Have proper foul-weather kit for all crew. Dry suits are excellent. Insulate all areas of the body, especially the high heat-loss areas: head, neck, armpits, sides of chest and groin. Keep warm and dry, but avoid sweating; wear layered clothes.
● Rotate watch frequently.
● Get plenty of rest, prevent fatigue.
● Eat and drink normally, *no alcohol.*
● Prevent dehydration; watch urine colour (drink more if colour becomes more intense).
● Avoid seasickness.
● Take into account special medical problems of crew members.
● Regularly train crew in Man Overboard recovery.
● Have two or more crew trained in CPR (Cardio-pulmonary Resuscitation).

SURVIVAL IN COLD WATER (under 75°F, 25°C)
(all UK waters)

● **If boat is in trouble**, put on dry or survival suits if carried. Radio for help; give position, number of crew, injuries, boat description. Make visual distress signals. Stay below if possible. Remain aboard until sinking is inevitable.
● **If going overboard**, launch life raft and EPIRB (Emergency Position Indicating Radio Beacon). Take grab bag, visual distress signals and waterproof hand-held VHF. Get into raft, stay out of water as water conducts heat out of the body 20 times faster than air. Remain near boat if practicable.
● **If in the water**, crew should stay together near the boat. This makes everyone easier to find, helps morale. Enter life raft, keep dry suit or survival suit on if worn.
● **If not wearing dry suit or survival suit**, make sure you wear a lifejacket, keep clothes and shoes on for some insulation and flotation. Keep hat on to protect head. Get all or as much of body out of water as soon as possible – into raft or swamped boat or onto flotsam. Avoid swimming or treading water, which increases heat loss. Minimise exposed body surface. A splashguard accessory on the lifejacket greatly improves resistance to swallowing seawater and also accommodates involuntary "gasping" when plunged into cold water.

Reproduced by kind permission of US Sailing , Box 209, Newport, RI 02840 and Richard Clifford

F°	C°	
99.6°	37.6°	**NORMAL**
97°	36°	**MILD** Condition
93°	34°	**MODERATE** Condition
90°	32°	**SEVERE** Condition
82°	28°	**CRITICAL** Condition

Body temperature (taken rectally)

RANGES OF
HYPOTHERMIA SYMPTOMS

Note: Most physical symptoms vary with each individual and may be unreliable indicators of core body temperature. Only a low temperature rectal thermometer gives reliable core temperature (the mouth cools too rapidly). In general, as body temperature fails, symptoms will increase.

HYPOTHERMIA FIRST AID

ALL CASES
- Keep victim horizontal
- Move victim to dry, shelter and warmth
- Allow to urinate from horizontal position
- Handle gently
- Remove wet clothes – cut off if necessary
- Apply mild heat (comfortable to your skin) to head, neck, chest and groin – use hot water bottles, warm moist towels
- Cover with blankets or sleeping bag; insulate from cold – including head and neck
- Report to Doctor by radio

MILD CONDITIONS
(97-93°F, 36-34°C)
- Shivering, cold hands and feet
- Still alert and able to help self
- Numbness in limbs, loss of dexterity, clumsiness
- Pain from cold

MILD CASES
- Primary task is to prevent further heat loss and allow body to rewarm itself
- Give warm, sweet drinks – *no alcohol – no caffeine*
- Apply mild heat source to stabilise temperature and/or
- Re-heat to point of perspiring
- Keep victim warm and horizontal for several hours

MODERATE CONDITIONS
(93-90°F, 34-32°C)
- Same as above
- Confusion, loss of time estimation and reasoning power

MODERATE CASES
- Same as above
- Offer sips of warm liquid only if victim is fully conscious and able to swallow without difficulty – *no alcohol – no caffeine*
- Have victim checked by doctor

SEVERE CONDITIONS
(90-82°F, 32-28°C)
- Shivering decreases or stops
- Further loss of reasoning and recall, confusion, abnormal behaviour
- Victim appears drunk; very clumsy, slurs speech, denies problem and may resist help
- Unable to help themselves
- Victim semiconscious to unconscious
- Muscular rigidity increasing

SEVERE CASES
- Obtain medical advice as soon as possible using your radio
- Assist victim, but avoid jarring him – rough handling may cause cardiac arrest or ventricular fibrillation of heart
- No food or drink
- Observe for vomiting and be prepared to clear airway
- *Ignore pleas of "Leave me alone, I'm OK" victim is in serious trouble* – keep continuous watch over victim
- Lay victim down in bunk, wedge in place, elevate feet, keep immobile; no exercise
- Apply external mild heat to head, neck, chest and groin – keep temperature from dropping, but avoid too rapid a temperature rise

---

CRITICAL CONDITIONS
(82°F, 28°C and below)
- Unconscious, may look dead
- Little or no apparent breathing
- Pulse slow and weak, or no pulse found
- Skin cold, may be bluish-grey colour
- Very rigid

CRITICAL CASES
- *Always assume the patient is revivable – hypothermic victims may look dead – don't give up – pulse very difficult to feel, breathing may have stopped*
- Handle with extreme care
- Tilt the head back to open the airway – look, listen and feel for breathing and pulse for one or two full minutes
- If there is any breathing or pulse, no matter how faint or slow, do not give CPR, but keep a close watch on vital sign changes
- Stabilise temperature with available heat sources, such as naked chest to back warming by other crew member (leave legs alone)
- *If no breathing or pulse for one or two minutes, begin CPR immediately. Do not give up until victim is thoroughly warm – alive or dead.*
- *Medical help imperative – hospitalisation needed*

WARNING
- First aid for severe and critical hypothermia is to add heat to stabilise temperature only. Rapid rewarming, such as a hot shower or bath, may be fatal; it will, at least, cause complications. Allow body to rewarm itself slowly.
- Body core temperature lags behind skin temperature during rewarming. Keep victim protected for extended period after apparent full recovery or medical help arrives. *Many hours are required for full return to normal temperature even though victim says he has recovered.*
- Always assume hypothermia is present in all man overboard situations in which victim has been exposed for more than 10–15 minutes
- Victims may also be suffering from near drowning, thus needing oxygen. Observe for vomiting.
- In a helicopter rescue, protect victim – including the head – from rotor blast wind chill

APPENDIX F
DROGUES AND SEA ANCHORS

TERMINOLOGY

The term "drogue" generally means a device dragged from the stern of a vessel which continues to make steerage way through the water but at reduced speed. The term "sea anchor" generally means a device streamed from the bows of a vessel practically halted in the water by the action of the sea anchor.

LIFERAFTS

Every liferaft has a sea anchor supplied as part of its equipment. A sea anchor is critical to the safe use of a liferaft and dramatically reduces the chance of liferaft capsize. Its secondary function is to limit drift. A spare sea anchor may be carried in a grab bag. Sea anchors in liferafts should comply with ISO 17339 and the opportunity should be taken at service intervals to ensure this.

DROGUES ON YACHTS

A number of research programs have been conducted including one for the RORC by the Southampton University Wolfson Unit. In tests drogue deployment repeatedly prevented typical yacht forms from being slewed sideways and rolled in heavy breaking seas.

Deployment of a drogue over the stern means that heavy water will break over that part of the yacht, so all openings must be properly secured shut.

A "series-drogue" invented by Donald Jordan has the ability to continue to provide drag even if part of the device is "surfing" under a wave crest.

SEA ANCHORS ON YACHTS

The most common form of sea anchor for yachts is the "parachute" anchor developed from aviation parachutes. Specialist manufacturers have accumulated much data to demonstrate the effectiveness of the device which can enable a vessel to take seas bows-on, reduce drift to the order of one knot, and resist capsize.

ISAF Offshore Special Regulations Appendix F
Including US SAILING Prescriptions

SEA ANCHORS ON YACHTS

The most common form of sea anchor for yachts is the "parachute" anchor developed from aviation parachutes. Specialist manufacturers have accumulated much data to demonstrate the effectiveness of the device which can enable a vessel to take seas bows-on, reduce drift to the order of one knot, and resist capsize.

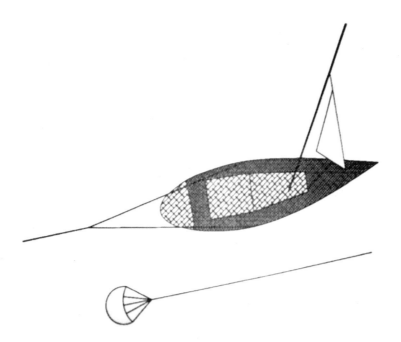

APPENDIX G
MODEL TRAINING COURSE
OFFSHORE PERSONAL SURVIVAL

With acknowledgements to IMO (International Maritime Organization), AYF (Australian Yachting Federation) and RYA (Royal Yachting Association) whose publications have been consulted in the preparation of this document.

INTRODUCTION

1   **Purpose of the model course.** To help provide training under ISAF Offshore Special Regulation Section 6. The model course is not the only means of providing such training. Other courses meeting the needs of Section 6 may apply to the appropriate MNA for ISAF Approval (see Introduction para 7).

2   **Use of the model course.** The chief instructor should review the experience and knowledge of the trainees before the course starts and revise details of the course plan accordingly. Trainees, who should have practical offshore sailing experience, should be encouraged to prepare for the course by familiarizing themselves with the topics in Special Regulations 6.02 and 6.03. See also the reading list in A 4.2. Particular skills (eg First Aid or professional medical knowledge) when suitably documented, may be accepted to excuse a trainee from that part of the course.

3   **Presentation.** The presentation may have to be repeated in various ways until the instructor is satisfied that the trainees have attained a good understanding of each topic.

4   **Evaluation.** The final activities on each day are examinations which should be used together with instructors' continuous assessments to provide a overall evaluation. The pass mark is to be taken as 60% in each of the marked units.

5   **Implementation.** Detailed requirements are given below. Thorough preparation is the key to successful implementation of the course.

6   **Structure of the model course.**

Part A describes the framework for the course, with aims and objectives and notes on suggested teaching facilities and equipment.

Part B provides an outline of lectures, and practical sessions. A suggested timetable is included but it is more important that trainees achieve proficiency in the required skills than that a strict timetable is followed.

Part C sets out the detailed syllabus.

7 ISAF Approved Training Courses and Trainee Certification.

7.1 The status of "ISAF Approved" together with authority to use the ISAF logo may only be awarded to a training course by an ISAF MNA (Member National Authority) who must be satisfied that the course delivers training as required by Special Regulation 6.01. A grant of approved status carries with it a duty on the MNA to ensure that the course provider continues to deliver appropriate training over the course of time. An annual review may be appropriate for this purpose. The MNA must remove approved status if and when it judges this necessary.

7.2 It is not necessary for a training course to follow Appendix G Model Training Course in order to receive approval as in 7.1 above. The overriding requirement is that the course must deliver the training required by Special Regulation 6.01.

7.2 An MNA which lacks experience in offshore training or for other reasons needs advice should contact the ISAF Offshore Training Advisory Panel via the ISAF office. The OTAP is appointed by and reports to the ISAF Offshore Special Regulations sub-committee.

7.3 A sailor holding an in-date "pass" certificate (each has a validity of 5 years) from an ISAF Approved Offshore Personal Survival Course shall be accepted by a race organizer as having complied with the requirements of ISAF Offshore Special Regulation 6.01.

7.4 "Pass" certificates issued at an ISAF Approved course shall carry the statement "ISAF Approved Offshore Personal Survival Course" and may carry the ISAF logo.

7.5 Unless otherwise stated in the Notice of Race, it is not mandatory that a training course for compliance with SR 6.01 is "ISAF Approved" however this status is encouraged wherever possible.

ISAF Offshore Special Regulations Appendix G
Including US SAILING Prescriptions

Part A Framework

A1 Class Size The maximum recommended class size is 20. When smaller work groups are established, this will allow for about four in each group. A suggested minimum number for the class would be ten. Otherwise it is difficult to promote discussion in smaller work groups.

A2 Instructors should have:
- wide experience of offshore sailing including sailing in severe weather
- a thorough knowledge of the course material
- a thorough knowledge of the requirements of the ISAF Offshore Special Regulations a good understanding of teaching methods

A3 Facilities and equipment

A 3.1 A suitable classroom is required with desks or tables and chairs. It should be possible to move the furniture around so that a variety of room arrangements can be used. Ideally, extra rooms will be available for when the class is split into groups, since each group should have a separate space in which to work.

A 3.2 The main room should be provided with the following equipment:
- a whiteboard or blackboard
- a flip chart
- writing materials for trainees
- an overhead projector (OHP) for transparencies
- a computer projector (with additional sound channel if not integral)
- a video tape player compatible with the computer projector
- a PC or laptop with CD-ROM drive, all compatible with the computer projector
- a reflective screen designed for use with the computer projector
- adequate electric sockets located so that the equipment can be positioned safely.

A 3.3 Group rooms should be provided with a table and chairs and some form of board and writing materials.

A 3.4 A video camera may be useful and should be compatible with the computer projector or alternatively must produce video tapes compatible with the video tape player.

A 3.5   A warm-water swimming pool with all appropriate safety equipment, personnel and facilities making it suitable for demonstration and training with lifejackets and liferafts. A wave-generator may provide added realism.

A 3.6   An outdoor location with appropriate safety equipment, personnel and facilities making it suitable for demonstration and training with pyrotechnics and fire extinguishers.

A4 Recommended Reference and Display Material
This section will be updated as information is submitted from MNAs. Course providers are encouraged to refer to materials relevant to their own areas of operation.

A 4.1   For the Instructors
Printed Material
- ISAF Offshore Special Regulations complete with separately-printed Appendices A2 (Liferafts) and G (the present document)
- ISAF RRS (The Racing Rules of Sailing)
- International Regulations for the Prevention of Collision at Sea
- Admiralty Summary of Notices to Mariners (NP 247)
- IAMSAR (International Aeronautical and Maritime Search and Rescue) manual, or manual for small craft (in preparation)
- ALRS (Admiralty List of Radio Signals) Volume 5 GMDSS (NP 285)
- SOLAS (Safety of Life At Sea Convention) Consolidated Edition
- International Life-Saving Appliance (LSA) Code
  Appropriate ISAF MNA Training Booklet or if none, at least one of
- RYA Practical Course Notes on Sea Survival
- AYF equivalent
- US Sailing Equivalent

Video Tapes
A Highway of Low Pressure

CD-ROMs
COSPAS-SARSAT

A 4.2   For the Trainees

A 4.2.1 Possession of:
- ISAF Offshore Special Regulations
- ISAF RRS (The Racing Rules of Sailing)
- International Regulations for the Prevention of Collision at Sea
- Admiralty Summary of Notices to Mariners (NP 247)
- IAMSAR (International Aeronautical and Maritime Search and Rescue) manual, or manual for small craft (in preparation).
- First Aid at Sea (Justins and Berry, published Adlard Coles) or equivalent
- Appropriate ISAF Member National Authority Training Booklet or if none, at least one of
- RYA Practical Course Notes on Sea Survival
- AYF equivalent
- US Sailing Equivalent

A 4.2.2 Knowledge of:
- ALRS (Admiralty List of Radio Signals) Volume 5 GMDSS (NP 285)
- SOLAS (Safety of Life At Sea Convention) Consolidated Edition
- International Life-Saving Appliance (LSA) Code
- International Medical Guide for Ships (WHO, World Health

A 4.2.3 Recommended further study:
The Grab Bag Book (F & M Howorth, Adlard Coles)
Instant Weather Forecasting (A Watts, Adlard Coles)
Heavy Weather Sailing (A Coles & P Bruce, Adlard Coles)
Essentials of Sea Survival (F Golden and M Tipton, Human Kinetics)

ISAF Offshore Special Regulations Appendix G
Including US SAILING Prescriptions

Part B Outline Timetable *(2 pages)*

Part C Detailed Syllabus
paragraph numbers refer to session numbers in Part B

Session 1 Introduction

1.0 The instructor gives an overview of the course and administrative arrangements, and explains the assessment and exam procedures. If the course has ISAF Approval (see introduction para 7) the certificate will be so endorsed. The instructor should also deliver a final course timetable.

1.1 The importance of training both in formal sessions and also as part of the routine in running a sailing yacht.

1.2 The importance of a "safety ethos"

1.3 The crew brief including safety equipment, stowage details, emergency procedures, responsibilities and how to send a Mayday call and use EPIRB and flares in case the skipper and key crew members are incapacitated. Show stowage chart required in Special Regulations: crew experience and fitness must be adequate

1.4 Responsibility of skipper for safe conduct of vessel and oversight and direction of crew actions. Responsibility of crew members for their own safety and in the discharge of their duties, to contribute to the safety of the vessel and the rest of the crew.

Session 2 Care and maintenance of safety and other equipment

2.1 Routine to check, service, clean, dry, fit and adjust to wearer, and correctly store safety equipment. Give examples eg safety harness , inflatable lifejackets, liferafts etc.

2.2 Checks to continue under way including eg rigging (pins in place and undistorted, wires not fractured, running rigging not unduly chafed, shackles seized when appropriate), seacocks, stern gland, toilet plumbing, etc.

2.3 Availability of reserve navigation lights and general spares.

2.4 Marking of floating equipment with vessel name.

2.5 Check and overhaul dan buoy, jon buoy, MoB modules, lifeslings etc.

2.6 Understand that dormant water or dirt in a fuel tank may be kicked up and taken into the engine in very rough weather - ensure that engine oil and fuel filler caps etc are kept clean and secure.

ISAF Offshore Special Regulations Appendix G
Including US SAILING Prescriptions

Session 3 Storm sails

3.1 Storm and heavy-weather sails including those on board the trainee's boat.

3.2 How are they set?

3.3 Where are they stowed?

3.4 Importance of practicing from time to time even in light weather.

3.5 Understand the changed pressures on the rig when using reduced sail in very heavy weather.

3.6 Dangers of heavy water breaking over the boat and carrying away poorly-stowed sails and sails set too low down.

3.7 Danger of heavy metal shackles in storm sails

3.8 Importance of bright colour in storm sails.

3.9 Value (in some boats) of lashing down the main boom in heavy weather and setting a trysail without the boom.

Session 4 Damage Control and Repair

4.1 Plan to minimize damage in forthcoming heavy weather

4.2 Remedial action including use of spare materials and tools to cope with:-

    .1 loss of rudder/steering

    .2 loss of mast

    .3 flooding due to (a) collision damage forward, (b) amidships, (c) aft (d) seacock failure

    .4 stranding

    .5 severe weather damage eg (a) hatch ripped off, (b) coachroof split

    .6 loss of keel and/or capsize

    .7 collision with another vessel, a submerged object (eg container), sea life, etc.

ISAF Offshore Special Regulations Appendix G
Including US SAILING Prescriptions

Session 5 Heavy Weather – crew routines, boat handling, drogues

5.1   Detailed examination of risks, solutions and contingency plans including crew routines for:-

.1 general working in exposed positions – hooking on before leaving hatchway, remaining hooked on at all times (dual hooking), telling someone when going forward, when lifejackets and harnesses shall be worn, value of personal EPIRBs (PLBs) especially with on-board D/F

.2 preparation for rough weather – secure stowage for moving items.

.3 ensure jackstays rigged

.4 rough weather operations

.5 severe weather strategies

.6 galley operations lee strops, preparing hot food in thermos containers in advance of heavy weather

.7 importance of high visibility of yacht in heavy seaway: display of orange surface, use of white light or strobe light on deck or in rig (also of use on a dull day) consider flying radar reflector if robust type.

5.2   boat handling in a seaway noting in particular helming techniques and effect of conditions on boat and crew taking into account:-

.1 strength of wind

.2 duration of high wind

.3 length of fetch

.4 wave pattern

.5 definition of wave height and length including assessment methods

.6 wave refraction

.7 multiple wave patterns

.8 waves in tidal/current conditions

.7 predicting dangerous wave conditions

.10 angle of boat to a seaway and to individual waves

.11 early sail changes, sail change procedures, knowing the boat and its characteristics and tendencies

.12 heaving-to

.13 assessing options eg to stand off or cross a barred entrance

5.3   Effect of a drogue on a boat in severe weather

ISAF Offshore Special Regulations Appendix G
Including US SAILING Prescriptions

Session 6 Man overboard prevention and recovery

6.1 Prevention
.1 lifelines to be maintained in accordance with Special Regs
.2 harness to be clipped on at night and in rough weather (see C5.1.1)
.3 drawback of plain harness hooks
.4 harness crotch straps prevent "slip-out"
.5 use the sea toilet in bad weather not the stern

6.2 Recovery
.1 well-drilled routine (see Special Regulations Appendix D)
.2 "Mayday" on radio is valid if necessary
.3 quickly accessible hoisting rig
.4 value of horizontal lift and retention of horizontal position
.5 procedure and team ready to re-clothe, re-warm and check recovered person for injury, advising shore if necessary
.6 use of whistle, SOLAS-type lifejacket light, strobe light.

Session 7 Giving Assistance to other craft

7.1 Legal and rules requirements
.1 SOLAS obligations apply to all ships on all voyages**
.2 Racing Rules of Sailing**
.3 moral imperative
.4 communications obligations**
.5 log-keeping obligations**

**see supplement one (below)

7.2 manouevring close to a vessel sinking
.1 keep other vessel and shore informed
.2 be prepared to recover personnel from the water or a liferaft
.3 tactics if other vessel is on fire
7.3 understand that another yacht may be the only source of help..
7.4 towing and being towed

Session 8 Hypothermia

8.1 Actively counter its development by wearing proper protective clothing
8.2 Know the symptoms- shivering, irritability, lethargy, stumbling, slurred speech, loss of memory, victim feels cold, looks pale, breathing slow, pulse weak, leading to collapse and unconsciousness.
8.3 treatment - see First Aid at Sea by Justins and Berry or other textbook
8.4 do not – give alcohol, rub the skin to warm, or give up resuscitation.
8.5 value of immersion suits, thermal protective aids (TPAs)

Session 9 SAR organisation and methods

9.1 with regard to the SAR authorities in the areas sailed, know:

.2 their landline number to advise them of passage planning if appropriate

.3 how to call them in emergency

.4 what facilities they have (and don't have)

.5 if helicopters are in use, know the sea-rescue system (hi-line, basket pick-up, winchman bridle, etc.) and whether a pick-up from a deck, in the water, or in a liferaft is preferred

.6 know what radio frequency to expect to use for direct contact

.7 know what fixed-wing aircraft may be deployed

.8 understand fixed-wing search patterns, signal flares

.9 have a knowledge of global SAR organization

.10 how to cope with rescue attempts from passing ships

.11 knowledge of new IAMSAR for small craft

Session 10   Weather Forecasting

10.1   sources of weather forecasts

10.2   terms and definitions and their exact meaning

10.3   Beaufort wind scale compared with mph (statute miles per hour) and speed in knots (nautical miles per hour), and sea state scale.

10.4   logging own weather observations of cloud, wind, sea, barometer, sea temperature (sometimes critical) and air temperature, etc.: making own deductions

10.5   be prepared for local abnormalities

ISAF Offshore Special Regulations Appendix G
Including US SAILING Prescriptions

Session 11 Liferafts and Lifejackets (theory)

11.1	**Liferafts (theory)**
11.1.2	knowledge of liferaft standards: SOLAS, ISAF Appendix A Part 2 and ORC.
11.1.3	stowage, care and servicing of liferafts
11.1.4	liferaft emergency packs
11.1.5	grab bag contents and application
11.1.6	two key elements in combating liferaft capsize – drogue, ballast water pockets
11.1.7	the capsize mechanism and the re-righting procedure
11.1.8	when and how to launch a liferaft
11.1.9	protecting a liferaft in the minimum time it is alongside after launch
11.1.10	boarding a liferaft if possible dry: use of dry suits if possible
11.1.11	boarding a liferaft from the water: importance of boarding ramp and grab lines
11.1.12	crew organization both before boarding and within liferaft:: signalling for help, watchkeeping, damage repair, medical, water, food, keeping up morale, psychology of survival.
11.1.13	knowledge of physiological shock of cold water and hypothermia (see session 8) and its effect on human performance in tasks like liferaft operation and survival.
11.1.14	use of SART (optional in grab bag).

Session 11.2 Lifejackets (theory)

11.2.1	Understand the terminology in your part of the world: know the difference between a 150N lifejacket (or equivalent title) capable of turning over an unconscious person in the water to the face-up position within 30 seconds, and a lesser device which may only aid buoyancy.
11.2.2	Understand the accessories required in Special Regulations: whistle, marine-grade retro-reflective material, yacht's or wearer's name
11.2.3	Understand the accessories and attributes recommended in Special Regulations: light in accordance with the SOLAS LSA code, compliance with EN376 or near equivalent, crotch strap, splash guard
11.2.3	Know the relative merits and methods of use of all-inflatable buoyancy and part-fixed, part-inflatable, automatic inflation, gas inflation on demand, mouth-only inflation.
11.2.3	Know the importance of a good fit, lifejacket organized for quick donning, compatibility with harness.

Session 12   **Exam (1)**

This exam is one of two. Time for answering questions -about 15 minutes, with 5 minutes for marking after swapping the papers amongst the class. . Questions should be set to be answered quickly, eg multiple-choice, with at least two questions needing some narrative or listing. Overall assessment for the course will be a combination of the two exams plus the tutors' assessments during class and practical work. (See introduction para 4)

Session 13   **Liferafts and Lifejackets (practical)**

.1 a pool with a wave-making facility will add realism

.2 trainees to don shirt and trousers plus oilskins and to try swimming first without, then with 150N lifejackets. Majority of exercises with all trainees wearing 150N lifejackets.

.3 inflate a liferaft and transfer a full complement into the raft (a) from the poolside (b) from the water (show difference between boarding with ramp and without): paddle the liferaft for a distance.

.4 capsize a liferaft and have each trainee right the raft whilst swimming

.5 trainees to haul into a raft one survivor who plays helpless

.6 in fully-loaded raft trainees to check out all equipment, including that in grab bag, deploying or using everything including food and water.

.7 trainee to attempt heliograph signalling (using spotlight in roof) from liferaft (more difficult if in wave-making pool).

.8 trainees to operate WT VHF hand-held and WT hand-held GPS talking to instructor as if a rescue vessel.

.9 trainees to try lifejackets both with and without crotch straps in place.

.10 each trainee to experience use of the splashguard in wave conditions.

.11 group to investigate ability of lifejacket to self-right.

.12 forming circle in water to aid visibility/morale – HELP/Huddle techniques

.13 towing an unconscious person

.14 assistance using throwing line to recover nearby survivor

.15 the opportunity of using the pool may be taken to demonstrate MoB modules, Lifeslings, lifebuoys etc.

.16 if a darkened pool is available, demonstrate retro-reflective tape.

.17 trainees who depend on spectacles may consider having an indestructible pair as part of their personal survival kit.

ISAF Offshore Special Regulations Appendix G
Including US SAILING Prescriptions

Sessions 14/15   Fire precautions and fire fighting (theory and practical)

.1 fire theory

.2 most common causes of fire in small craft

.3 prevention

.4 equipment – fire extinguishers, fire blankets, services, tested, maintained, fit for purpose. Advantages/disadvantages of various types of extinguisher.

.5 practical operation of fire extinguishers (actual fire is not required in this training course)

Sessions 16/17   CPR and First Aid (theory and practice)

.1 the ABC code (Airway – Breathing – Circulation -see First Aid at Sea by Justins and Berry).

.2 practical application of chest compressions and mouth-to-mouth breaths on purpose-built dummy.

.3 how to deal with bleeding and shock

.4 breathing difficulty and choking (asphyxia)

.5 burns and scalds

.6 drowning

.7 positioning and care of casualty including in evacuation by boat or helicopter

.8 fractures and sprains

.9 sudden illness: heart attack, heatstroke, seasickness, stroke, head injuries.

.10 wounds and injuries

.11 importance of knowing medical problems if any of crew members before sailing.

.12 seasickness

.13 knowledge of contents of standard first-aid kit

.14 how to get medical advice by radio

ISAF Offshore Special Regulations Appendix G
Including US SAILING Prescriptions

Sessions 18/19   Communications equipment (VHF, GMDSS, satcomms)
(theory and practical)

.1   VHF main installations and hand-helds.
.2   Special Regulations requirements for VHF 25W output, masthead
      aerial, emergency aerial.
.3   SSB (still in use though now without the large number of
      marine shore stations).
.4   Satcoms: A, B, C, D and M. Non-INMARSAT types (eg Iridium).
.5   Terrestrial cellphones. Limitations.
.6   GMDSS, DSC, AIS.
.7   Aviation VHF and its use in SAR.
.8   Obligation to log communications connected with distress
      working**

**see Supplement

Sessions 20/21   Pyrotechnics and EPIRBs (theory and practical)

.1 pyrotechnics required in Special Regulations: hand flares, parachute flares,
smoke signals. Usage, precautions, range of visibility, duration, behavior in
high winds, altitude of parachute flares and avoiding conflict with aircraft,
different operating mechanisms.
.2 stowage of pyrotechnics including some for ready use.
.3 use of white flares
.4 understand the operation of the 406 MHz EPIRB and its ancillary 121.5
beacon; the phasing out of 121.5 MHz as a distress alert system but its use in
local area homing by SAR units and yachts with special-purpose D/F
receivers on board in conjunction with 121.5 units known as PLBs.
.5 understand the operation of the INMARSAT type "E" EPIRB.
.6 understand the operation of ARGOS-type beacons.
.7 understand the integration of distress beacons in the GMDSS framework.

Session 22   Exam (2)

This exam is one of two. Time for answering questions -about 15 minutes, with 5
minutes for marking after swapping the papers amongst the class. . Questions should
be set to be answered quickly, eg multiple-choice, with at least two questions needing
some narrative or listing. Overall assessment for the course will be a combination of
the two exams plus the tutors' assessments during class and practical work. (See
Introduction para 4 for marking details).

ISAF Offshore Special Regulations Appendix G
Including US SAILING Prescriptions

Supplement One

1 The Racing Rules of Sailing state:-

"1 SAFETY
1.1 Helping Those in Danger
A boat or competitor shall give all possible help to any person or vessel in danger"

2 SOLAS Convention Chapter V
Regulation 33 (replaces old Regulation 10) states:-

"The master of a ship at sea which is in a position to be able to provide assistance, on receiving a signal from any source that persons are in distress at sea, is bound to proceed with all speed to their assistance, if possible informing them or the SAR service that the ship is doing so. If the ship receiving the distress alert is unable or, in the special circumstances of the case, considers it unreasonable or unnecessary to proceed to their assistance, the master must enter in the log-book the reason for failing to proceed to the assistance of the persons in distress and, taking into account the recommendations of the Organization++, inform the appropriate SAR service accordingly.
++Refer to the immediate action to be taken by each ship on receipt of a distress message in the IAMSAR Manual, as it may be amended."

Reference to the original text and its context is strongly recommended.

3 Annual Summary of Admiralty Notices to Mariners NP 247 1-22
Section 4 states:-

"The radio watch on the international distress frequencies, which certain classes of ships are required to keep when as sea, is one of the most important factors in the arrangements for the rescue of people in distress at sea, and every ship should make its contribution to safety by guarding one or more of these distress frequencies for as long as is practicable whether or not required to do so by regulation."

APPENDIX H
ISAF Code for the organization of Oceanic Races

The following Code was approved by the Council of the International Sailing Federation in November 1999.

1. Organizers of oceanic races shall should consult with the SAR (Search and Rescue) authorities through whose areas a race is proposed to pass.

2. All yachts shall be equipped to standards which at least comply with the relevant level of Special Regulations as adopted by ISAF, class rules notwithstanding.

3. In accordance with Special Regulations, an adequate number of competitors on each yacht shall have survival training.

4. Races shall be conducted in compliance with the ISAF Racing Rules of Sailing and the COLREGS whenever it is appropriate for these rules and regulations to be applied.

An Oceanic Race is defined as any offshore race over 800 miles.

ISAF Offshore Special Regulations Appendix J
Including US SAILING Prescriptions

APPENDIX J
CATEGORY 5 SPECIAL REGULATIONS
for inshore races

Category 5 Special Regulations are intended for use in short races, close to shore in relatively warm and protected waters where adequate shelter and/or effective rescue is available all along the course, held in daylight only.
With the exception of recommended item 3.14 pulpits etc. for which see the main body of Special Regulations, all the items relevant to Category 5 are shown in Appendix J.
US SAILING prescriptions are printed in bold italic letters.

Category 5
A - Basic
The following regulations shall be observed:-

Regulation	Item
1.02	**Responsibility of the person in charge** The Safety of a yacht and her crew is the sole and inescapable responsibility of the owner, or owner's representative who must do his best to ensure that the yacht is fully found, thoroughly seaworthy and manned by an experienced crew who have undergone appropriate training and are physically fit to face bad weather. He must be satisfied as to the soundness of hull, spars, rigging, sails and all gear. He must ensure that all safety equipment is properly maintained and stowed and that the crew know where it is kept and how it is to be used.
2.03.1	**suitability of equipment** All equipment required by Special Regulations shall:- a) function properly b) be regularly checked, cleaned and serviced c) when not in use be stowed in conditions in which deterioration is minimised d) be readily accessible e) be of a type, size and capacity suitable and adequate for the intended use and size of the yacht.
3.08	**hatches & companionways** 3.08.1 No hatch forward of the maximum beam station shall open inwards excepting ports having an area of less than 0.071m2 (110 sq in). 3.08.2 A hatch shall be: a) so arranged as to be above the water when the hull is heeled 90 degrees

Regulation	Item
	b) permanently attached c) capable of being firmly shut immediately, and remaining firmly shut in a 180 degree capsize (inversion) 3.08.3 A companionway hatch extending below the local sheerline, shall: a) not be permitted in a yacht with a cockpit opening aft to the sea (3.09.6) b) be capable of being blocked off up to the level of the local sheerline, provided that the companionway hatch shall continue to give access to the interior with the blocking devices (e.g. washboards) in place 3.08.4 A companionway hatch shall: a) be fitted with a strong securing arrangement which shall be operable from the exterior and interior including when the yacht is inverted b) have any blocking devices i) capable of being retained in position with the hatch open or shut ii) whether or not in position in the hatchway, secured to the yacht (e.g. by lanyard) for the duration of the race, to prevent their being lost overboard iii) permit exit in the event of inversion
3.09	cockpits 3.09.1 cockpits shall be structurally strong, self-draining quickly by gravity at all angles of heel and permanently incorporated as an integral part of the hull. 3.09.2 cockpits must be essentially watertight, that is, all openings to the hull must be capable of being strongly and rigidly secured 3.09.3 a bilge pump outlet pipe or pipes shall not be connected to a cockpit drain 3.09.4 A cockpit sole shall be at least 2% LWL above LWL (or in IMS yachts first launched before 1/03, at least 2% L above LWL) 3.09.5 a bow, lateral, central or stern well shall be considered a cockpit for the purposes of 3.09 3.09.6 In cockpits opening aft to the sea structural openings aft shall be not less in area than 50% maximum cockpit depth x maximum cockpit width

ISAF Offshore Special Regulations Appendix J
Including US SAILING Prescriptions

Regulation	Item
	3.09.7 Cockpit volume i) age or series date before 4/92:- the total volume of all cockpits below lowest coamings shall not exceed 9% (LWL x maximum beam x freeboard abreast the cockpit). ii) age or series date 4/92 and after:- as in (i) above except that "lowest coamings" shall not include any aft of the FA station and no extension of a cockpit aft of the working deck shall be included in calculation of cockpit volume iii) IMS-rated boats may use instead instead of LWL, maximum beam, freeboard abreast the cockpit; the IMS terms L, B and FA.
3.09.8	Cockpit drains Cockpit drain cross section area (after allowance for screens if fitted) shall be:- i) in yachts with earliest of age or series date before 1/72 or in any yacht under 8.5m (28ft) LOA - at least that of 2 x 25mm (one inch) unobstructed openings or equivalent ii) in yachts with earliest of age or series date 1/72 and later - at least that of 4 x 20mm (3/4 inch) unobstructed openings or equivalent
	US SAILING prescribes that cockpit drains shall be accessible for cleaning
4.01.1	sail numbers Yachts which are not in an ISAF International Class or Recognized Class shall comply with RRS 77 and RRS Appendix G as closely as possible, except that sail numbers allotted by a State authority are acceptable.

Category 5
B - Portable Equipment
The following shall be provided:-

Regulation	Item
3.23.5 (e)	one manual bilge pump
3.23.5 (f)	one bucket of stout construction with at least 9 litres (2 UK gallons, 2.4 US gallons) capacity plus a lanyard
3.24.1 (b)	one compass (a hand-held is acceptable)
4.05.1	one fire extinguisher required if electrical system, engine or stove on board
4.05.1	one fire extinguisher required if electrical system, engine or stove on board
4.06.1	one anchor
4.17	yacht's name on buoyant equipment
4.22.1 (a)	a lifebuoy with a drogue, or a lifesling without a drogue. Marine grade retro-reflective tape shall be fitted.
	US SAILING prescribes that the lifebuoy must be inherently buoyant
4.24	a heaving line shall be provided of length 15m-25m (50ft-75ft) readily accessible to the cockpit or helm
	US SAILING prescribes that the heaving line be of 1/4 in. (6mm) minimum diameter, floating UV-inhibited and ready accessible to the cockpit
5.01.1	each crew member shall have a lifejacket as follows: (a) equipped with a whistle (b) fitted with marine grade retro-reflective tape (d) if inflatable, regularly checked for air retention (e) clearly marked with yacht's or wearer's name
	US SAILING prescribes for Category 5 lifejackets as above or US Coast Gaurd approved Type III personal Floating devices

ISAF Offshore Special Regulations Appendix J
Including US SAILING Prescriptions

Category 5
C - Recommendations

Regulation	Item
3.14	sail numbers for display when sails are down
4.01.2	a flashlight
4.07.1 (a)	pulpits, stanchions, lifelines -see main text of Special Regulations 3.14 etc.
4.08.2	a first aid kit
4.11.1	a waterproof chart
4.13	an echo sounder or lead line
4.16	tools and spare parts
4.24	a "throwing sock" type of heaving line - see Appendix D
4.26.9	mainsail reefing to reduce the luff by at least 60%, or a storm trysail as in 4.26.6.
5.01.2	lifejacket equipment or attribute: (a) a lifejacket light in accordance with SOLAS LSA code 2.2.3 (white, >0.75 candelas, > 8 hours) (b) at least 150N buoyancy, arranged to securely suspend an unconscious man face upwards at approximately 45 degrees to the water surface, in accordance with EN396 or near equivalent (c) a crotch strap or thigh straps (d) a splashguard: see EN394. (e) if inflatable, supplied with a compressed gas inflation system
	US SAILING recommends either a Type 1 U.S. Coast Guard approved personal floatation device or an inflatable personal floatation device meeting the definition in the above paragraph. Each inflatable device should be inflated and inspected annually. Service dates shall be marked on floatation devices.
	US SAILING prescribes that all personnel on deck shall wear personal floatation while starting and finishing without exception, and at all other times except when the Captain of the boat directs that it may be set aside.
	US SAILING note: As is true of all of these regulations. The prescriptions above do not necessarily replace the requirements of the other governing authorities.

NOTES

ISAF Special Regulations Governing Offshore and Oceanic Equipment and Preparation
Including US SAILING Prescriptions

NOTES

NOTES

NOTES